I'LL CARRY MY OWN GROCERIES THANK YOU

Connecting with your aging parents and adult children to live happier, healthier lives together.

CATHY EWING

DEDICATION

To the women of my family -
you are shining examples of fearless, strong, creative, and loving women:
my mother, Lois, Aunt Edith, Aunt Christina (Teenie), Aunt Joanna
(Honey), Aunt Elaine, Linda, Kathy, and Vickie. Let's not forget Evie,
Norma, and Diane, who I consider family.
I was watching.

To my husband, Brent - thank you for supporting all of my crazy ideas.
I love you.

CONTENTS

	Acknowledgments	i
1	Choosing to Live Close	1
2	The Nature of Friendship	5
3	Creating Verbal Connections	11
4	Ways to Practice Being Friends	17
5	Finding Time	21
6	Being Social with Family Makes Us Bolder	25
7	Chores are Activity – Get Your Fitbit	31
8	Exercise Together	37
9	Outdoor Activities Putting Fear in Its Place	43
10	When You Are Really Scared Think of Us	49
11	Getting Creative	53
12	Community Events	61
13	Connecting to the Family Tree	65
14	Other Ways to Share the Past	75
	Sources	81
	About the Generation Gals	83
	A Place for Notes and Activities	84

ACKNOWLEDGMENTS

My year-long experiment happened because my daughter, Caitlyn, and mother, Lois, were willing guinea pigs. Thank you for supporting my quest for a healthier and happier life. My life is better because you became my Generation Gals.

I could not have finished writing this book without Deby, whose kind words and suggestions kept me going.

I hope you will use our suggestions in A Place for Notes, Ideas, and Activities at the back of the book to plan conversations and special times with those you love.

Ideas keep coming at www.generationgals.com.

ONE
CHOOSING TO LIVE CLOSE

As I move into my mid-fifties, I feel the need to be more intentional with my time. I am at that age where I look back and move forward – it's like walking along the edge of a lake enjoying the reflection. I am in the middle where the view ahead and the view back are the same distance.

My mother, at 87, is about thirty years older, and my daughter, at 23, is about thirty years younger than me. They are strong creative women - one showing me where I'm going and one reminding of where I've been. I have chosen to live close to my mother while we are still healthy and active. My daughter has chosen to live near me.

My friends lovingly talk about their parents in few ways: 1) I'm moving close to take care of my parents; 2) My parents are part of my daily plan – taking care of my yard or babysitting; 3) My parents are my heroes or friends. That's the beautiful thing about family – we take care of each other. I wanted more. I wanted our interactions to make each of us healthier.

My mother, daughter, and I decided to explore how we could intentionally 'be friends first.' Three women. Three generations. Generation Gals. We would strive together to be healthier, happier, more curious, and more connected. We would find ways to share emotional vulnerability – in the way best friends do. We would learn more about each other, going beyond the myths that come from old family stories and get real.

We chose to be active – each at our level of fitness. We chose to be curious – each selecting activities. We chose to learn something new – and share it. We chose to feed off of each other's strengths.

These are stories from our journey and information from the experts. We changed our interactions by trying new activities while being intentional with our communications. We hope this can be a guide for your journey. We created a series of maxims – not as rules but as reminders – to help us get the most from the time spent together.

Here we remind ourselves to do things with each other rather than just for each other and stoke our curiosity in the process.

Living Close.

At 87, my mother still lives life as an adventure. We lived apart for more than 35 years, spending vacations or visits together. I made a conscious decision to move near my mother while she was still well enough for us to experience an active life together.

When I first moved to Alaska, I remember making lunch for Mom and me. It was a salad with unusual summer vegetables, shrimp, and a light dressing. I set the table in the sun, poured glasses of wine, and invited her to join me. It felt so relaxed and yet so festive – I think Martha Stewart strives to help us have these moments – and Mom and I just chatted about the everyday moments of living. I loved that lunch because I knew that we were in a place where we would see each other much more often, and it felt good to be hanging out with a friend.

It only took a week for adventure to come our way. We were headed home down the two-mile trail by the house. It is canopied by birch and spruce trees with berry bushes and mounds of discarded seed husks. The trail travels along the mountain's ridge, changing from dry forest floor to soft beds of moss and from dense trees to thick shrubbery. Residents of the area have hung beautiful Christmas balls along the way, and our chairs sit under a giant birch at the trail's peak, offering a stunning view and comfortable rest. Everyone in the neighborhood hikes here often.

Mom and I were deep in conversation as we rounded a corner and almost walked into the young brown bear feasting on berries. I have never been that close to a bear before, even at the zoo, and stood stunned. Mom immediately raised her hands her head and started singing Christmas carols – loudly. I joined in, and we serenaded that bear with Jingle Bells, Deck the Halls, and Frosty the Snowman. He sat back on his haunches and faced us. I want to believe he was enjoying the show, even though I know he was just as frightened and concerned as we were at this chance encounter. Eventually, he turned and strolled off into the forest.

It was the first, and the last time we came face-to-face with a bear that close. It was thrilling and indicative of how our lives move from serene to challenging. While we don't go out of our way to include crazy adventures, we are always open to a new experience. A friend joked about the bear as a spirit guide for our future adventures. The bear is a symbol of strength and courage — and many other things — I enjoy believing that she is right to see the bear as a sign.

After five years in Fairbanks, my family moved to Anchorage, about 350 miles or six hours away. While Mom and I saw each other more often than when I lived outside of Alaska, it was not like being in the same town. I was doing many activities — skiing, hiking, running, going to the gym — alone.

Five years later, my job changed, and we moved back to Fairbanks. I am hoping for ten active years — she'd be 98 - and then ten less active years — she'd be 108. Just the other day, I saw a video of a 101-year-old woman who set a world record for the 100-yard dash in the Senior Olympics, so maybe all 20 years will be active.

TWO
THE NATURE OF FRIENDSHIP

Neighbors and acquaintances ask if they can adopt my mother, comparing their parental relationships to ours. Once, on a walk with my daughter, grandson, and mother, we were stopped by three groups of people who were so excited to see four generations out walking together.

I know I am lucky. Questioning the nature of friendship, and its role in our family began with two sets of hand weights and a YouTube video. A hyperactive British trainer in a cute aerobics outfit showed us how to get rid of batwings - that waddling fat under your upper arms. Mom and I began lifting little dumbbells for 20 minutes each night. We struggled with the weights equally and got better equally. I realized that we could do a workout together, and each of us would get healthier. We added yoga moves, golf moves, or moves from a magazine, but the talking, joking, sharing something new each night was so powerful for me.

Unfortunately, the closeness Mom and I were foraging left my relationship with my daughter behind. Wasn't I swapping time spent exercising alone to exercising with a partner? No. I was creating this intimate connection with someone else in front of my daughter, but not with my daughter. Not only was I enjoying this 'friendship time' with Mom, but I was also continually talking about it. I could see it was hurting Caitlyn, and being a problem solver with no empathy, invited her to "join us if you want." Her sorrow and my defensiveness came to a boiling point one afternoon, with both of us screaming our feelings while driving around in her small car. We got louder and louder, hoping the other would hear – until it was deafening!

It took me weeks of reflection to realize I was treating Caitlyn as a teenager rather than as an adult friend. I was expecting her to join the 'adults' rather than treating her as a friend and letting her lead.

The three of us began to have conversations about our future friendship and what we would like to do. We talked about how the experiences of our past shaped who we are today and how being eighty is just different than being fifty, which is different than being twenty. There were a few accusations of 'you don't understand' or 'you are not open to ideas,' but even those brought us closer.

It was much more difficult for me to relate to Caitlyn's suggestions because I could not put them in context. Many were social media related, and I did not want to invest time learning something new. I laugh now because the point of the Generation Gals experiment was for us to learn new things. For example, people around the world showed off four generations of their family. We didn't do it, but we should have. By not sharing our four generations, I believe I dimensioned Caitlyn's role and contributions to the group. I try to look forward rather than regretting the past, so I've lived and learned. Social media fun, here we come.

We began in earnest to explore the nature of friendship.

Do Family or Friends Make You Live Longer?

The answer is yes to both. Studies differ about whether friends are more critical or family is more important. They all agree that social interaction and emotional bonds lead to a longer, healthier life.

Growing older is something all of us do, so it is widely studied. Jeff Haden's article, "This Study of 300,000 People Reveals the 1 Secret to Living a Longer, Healthier Life, "[1] reviews an Australian study. That study determined that people with the most friends tended to outlive people with fewer friends by 22 percent. Also, the family didn't impact longevity. Researchers reviewed 150 studies that followed 300,000 individuals for an average of 7.5 years and found that individuals with strong social ties had a 50 percent better chance of survival.

On the other hand, a study from the University of Chicago found that people who had close relationships with family members lived longer than those with close relationships with friends. They asked 3,000 older individuals to write a list of five close connections. Those with more family members on the list tended to live longer.[2]

Nicola Conville, of bodyandsoul.com.au, points to a 2009 study from the Harvard Medical School that correlated a woman's number of friends with joyful lives. Women talk about their health to other women, yet they are not as proactive with their doctors. These conversations with female friends act as a catalyst for mental and physical health and well-being.[3]

Additional studies have found that engaging with friends leads to healthier behaviors, greater happiness, and fewer chronic illnesses.

If I can capture what makes us close as friends and apply it to what makes us close as family, all four of our generations will live longer, healthier lives.

The Concept of Care as a Verb.

Haden's article sums up his secret to living a longer, healthier life with the following observation.

"Casual friends see 'care' as a noun. Real friends see 'care' as a verb. They act on their feelings. They step in, step up, and sometimes step outside their comfort zone to do something selfless, just because they can. If you want to have closer friends [and I would add a more intimate family], make 'care' a verb. Support. Encourage. Help. And if you don't know how, ask — because real friends ask."

Can we care for an aging parent while being friends and flourish throughout our middle years?

Can we continue to grow as individuals because we are focusing on family relationships?

Can we do something now, so our kids look forward to having us close when we're 87 years old?

Can we improve our relationships with our adult children at the same time?

I did not do this for my father. I left the care and nurturing of him to my sister and his many friends. He passed away recently, and I have yet to deal with my feelings about myself for being so disconnected at the end. I hope something in this book will help you find ways to interact with your family as friends – making all of you happier and healthier.

Types of Friendships.

There are several different kinds of friendship – some casual and some close. Most of our associations are casual - time-based, interest-based, or transaction-based. Time-based friendships depend on where we are in our lives and our proximity: high school friends, college friends, neighbors, or the Mommy club. We are friends because we live close and are going through similar situations. We move on and most of these friends move into the category of an acquaintance or past friend. Social media has allowed us to reconnect and keep up with what these people are doing, but we are monitoring more than genuinely interacting.

Interest-based friendships develop because of a mutual interest and often form when we join a group. When I was a child, my mother joined the Flatirons Ski Club. This group hiked, biked, climbed, and skied together. They were very close-knit at the time, but eventually, they moved on to other things, and the club has an entirely different group of enthusiasts now. I have such fond memories of these people who introduced my mother and me to the outdoors. Quilting clubs, social clubs, even Karate or Yoga studios are home to these types of casual friends.

Transaction or mutual benefit-based friendships happen when both parties benefit from knowing each other. These are often business or work friendships. You remain friends or friendly over time and can immediately fall back into beneficial patterns when you are working together again. These are often opportunity-based, and the friendships change as the jobs change. Most of my friends are in this category because I love my work. These individuals feed my curiosity, take risks, and solve problems with me. They go for a drink with me but don't come too far into my personal life.

Getting Close.

True close friends are distinguished by a single trait – LOVE. I am blessed because I have a few close friends from my working past that made the transition into a close friendship. We shared heartbreaking times, divorces - death of parents, as well as wonderful times – boyfriends, marriages, children, grandchildren, and pets. We grew to love each other.

Women are more willing to share their feelings than men, creating a more intimate bond and greater vulnerability. This closeness when talking about experiences produces oxytocin, a 'feel-good' hormone that is good for us and makes us live longer.

My mother and I are not demonstratively emotional people by nature, but we share our vulnerabilities and go beyond surface emotions. We trust each other with those things that are our biggest concerns. My daughter wears her heart on her sleeve, being vulnerable to all that surrounds her. She engages with her emotions more actively. Recently I have found the beauty in her vulnerability and am working to be a little more like her.

I question my willingness to let Caitlyn change me. I hear myself dismissing her ideas – as they are leaving her lips. I correct her about things when I would not correct a friend. I want her to change me, so now I set down my suitcase of "I know better statements" before interacting.

When I see pictures of older women together, I understand the carefree nature of their laugh and everything that it represents. They are in the same emotional space sharing a lifetime of intimacy.

Finding Intimate Friendship with a Parent or Child.

There is something in the attraction between friends that is almost chemical. You see someone and are drawn to that person – a bonding of personalities and interests. This attraction also happens in families; however, it is not guaranteed. Some relationships need to build on a foundation of memories, curiosity, and time.

Here's the key. In a close friendship, both people gain by allowing the other to change them in unexpected ways, by being vulnerable and by being open. How do we set aside our baggage? How do we ignore some of the unwritten rules of our role as a parent, child, or grandchild so we can become real friends – happy, healthy, and fulfilled?

We need to set aside preconceived notions of the life we want for our children or our parents and bask in the happiness they have found for themselves. We help them; we do not force them. We recognize what is important to them, acknowledge it, and support it.

I will share how my Mom, my daughter, and I consciously nurtured these bonds over a year. There are ideas for activities that hopefully spur curiosity, lead to more significant understanding, and allow everyone in the relationship to be happier and healthier. This book discusses how we created a family connection and spent time being friends.

Throughout the journey, my daughter and I worked to define for ourselves this intimate friendship that transcends family connections, Caitlyn and I have become adult friends. The other day, I felt a shift from adult friends to intimate adult friends. We were discussing her medical issues, and she began sharing new insights about her situation: why it has changed over time and how she will continue to change in the future. The shift I felt was within myself. I switched from a directive parent – offering advice, making plans in my head, judging what was said, feeling responsible – to an intimate friend. The quality of my listening changed; I was interested and empathetic in a way I had never been before. The Mom role had dropped away, leaving room for my friendship to blossom. I'm guessing Caitlyn did not notice, but at the end of the conversation, I was glowing inside.

THREE
CREATING VERBAL CONNECTIONS

A good friend at work, Deby, and I were laughing about a funny Alaskan story, replete with bears, guns, fathers, city slicker boyfriends, and a whole lot of bad decision making. It was a story my mother told me the night before. Mom and I were rolling around on the floor – I mean doing the yoga portion of our workout – and sharing about our day. She was talking about her storytelling class and describing what made some of the people in the class great narrators. We stopped moving and just sat there laughing at these stories and dissecting what made an outstanding presentation.

Deby lamented that too many of the conversations with her mother bordered on the mundane. She wanted to create a connection, but often the discussion was about the washing machine repairman or being placed on hold. Her mother lives in a different state, so they always talk on the phone, and it is easier to struggle for conversation topics when you are not face-to-face. Add to this that they are talking less often, so there are fewer opportunities to get through the mundane to the meat. I thought back to conversations on the phone with family and how easy it was to be busy or distracted, but when you connected, it felt like you were in the room together.

I'm hoping the ideas below help set the stage for conversations that connect us, whether in person or long distance. Social media (Facebook, Instagram, or Snapchat) builds on relationships that already exist, but it cannot create or sustain a connection. I think of social media as the two-dimensional representation of a three-dimensional life. Conversation is where you share the third dimension – spontaneous two-way interaction.

Preparing to Connect.

I always wanted to be on committees with one particular faculty member when I worked at the University of Alaska Anchorage. This gentleman made me feel as if I were the most important person on earth when I was speaking. At first, I wondered if we had a psychic connection or past life relationship, and then I realized everyone in the meeting seemed to connect to him. I began to study his style so I could learn how to make everyone feel intelligent and heard.

The faculty member was a psychologist. He turned toward the speaker, not just his head, but his entire body focused on the person sharing. Then there were his non-verbal cues. He was listening and contemplating. His energy was focused on the speaker, and he was open to information. I have always wanted to be that type of listener – the person that makes you want to tell a story because you can see me listening.

So, how do we make this intense conversational connection happen with family? We almost know too much about each other; however, preparing to listen can change the entire conversation.

Here are some old tricks which work, in person or on the phone. If you know these already, think of them as gentle reminders.

Turn Toward the Speaker and Lean in Slightly.

When the conversation is moving around the table, you will be getting a workout for your waist. You don't want to flop around, but when someone is telling a story, sharing feelings or making a good point, stretch toward them.

Engage in the story by asking questions. Caitlyn often reminds me that I'm distracted or not listening by saying, "Well, I can see you don't care about this." I stop what I am doing and focus on her. From there, we decide if it is a topic worth our full attention. I believe we talk less about the mundane detritus of the day.

Stay in the present; do not start thinking about tomorrow or what to make for dinner. If the conversation is a repeat of one you had two days ago, or if it is too mundane, change the subject. I can't tell you the number of times I look back on a conversation and realize that I was going on and on about something which Mom doesn't care about at all. That was the time when we could have been connecting, and I wish she had just given me a hint – or verbal shove – in another direction.

Focus on the Other Person – Not What You Plan to Say Next.

I admit it; I am one of those people that can't wait to add on to what you are saying. I catch myself thinking about how my story or anecdote will build on what you are saying. It's a terrible habit. When I find myself doing this, I do not share my memory and guess what, we still connect without my scintillating contribution.

Apologize if You Talk Over Someone.

If the conversation is in a frenzy and everyone is engaged, don't feel guilty about interrupting because someone will probably talk over you too. However, if you are finishing someone's thoughts or running over them in normal conversation, apologize, and reset. I have to do this all the time. I want to solve the problem before I even know what the problem is or if they want my help.

Commonalities Make it Easy to Communicate.

Being curious makes commonalities easier to find. Mom and I talk about photography – her passion. We talk about stories – my passion. We talk about the crazy things people do – my daughter's passion. To build on commonalities, get tuned into what excites others and then explore to see if you can be excited too. We try to share a tidbit of information gleaned about one another's interest or latest project.

Psychologists Donn Byrne and Arthur Aaron study relationships. Byrne explains that people who agree with us validate our attitudes. Aaron believes that we also want to grow and expand as people and that qualities of others who are different promote growth if we can find common ground and expand our horizons benefiting from our differences.

Mom shows Caitlyn an article on a strange court case. We discuss the nature of criminals and the stupidity of some people. I forward photography tips to Mom. We'll dissect what makes a photo stunning or how an F stop works. Caitlyn suggests a place to hike or a place to go. She gives us ideas, even if she isn't planning to join us for the outing. We go to First Friday, an event held in many communities on the first Friday of every month that features art in unusual locations, like hair salons, or greenhouses. It's a scavenger hunt for art. Our participation not only shows we care, but we begin to create new areas of interest.

Open-ended Questions Lead to the Most Interesting Answers.

Closed-ended questions can be answered with a yes or no. for example, "How was your day?". Open-ended questions ask for more information and begin with 'describe,' 'tell me,' 'what,' or 'I wonder.'

I wonder a lot. I was talking about a character I'm developing for a book. This character loves to wear stylish women's boots, but he lives in a small village in Alaska. Mom, Caitlyn and I were thinking about living on the edge of society – when does being different go from individualistic to uncomfortable. What throws someone over that edge?

"There was a man who dressed in drag with full makeup. I would watch him from my window walking into town, but I never spoke to him," Mom says. Here she was a very young mother of two in a small town on the eastern plains of Colorado in the 1940s and 1950s. "I would never have spoken to him, but always assumed he had dressed up to see friends." I think about that conversation and that man often. When Mom told that story, it felt like I was peeking through the curtains to the woman she was in her twenties. It contrasts so starkly to Caitlyn, who grew up with drag on television because Rue Paul's Drag Race was a staple in our home and goes to live drag shows.

We all share more of these small remembrances from the past now. The new habit makes conversations more insightful and more interesting, and I want to believe it makes our minds healthier.

Finding the Real You.

It's the small things that can be humanizing. Discovering that my mother was not a good housekeeper when she was young was a revelation. My daughter struggles with housekeeping. When my mother started empathizing with her, I stopped looking at Caitlyn's housekeeping as a reflection of me as her mother. It made me see us all as individuals.

Growing up, I remember my mother as a rock – never uncertain, never afraid, and always ready with the answer. Now she shares how she felt in situations throughout her life. "I was so insecure when ... or I hated being patronized...or I remember crying in my office." Sharing these emotions helps your daughter or granddaughter as they are struggling with things in life. Rather than sharing what you did in certain situations, share what you felt. Feelings lead to close connections.

Books, games and the Sunday Jar.

Books, question games, or a Sunday Jar can lead to better conversations. These all have fun ideas for getting words flowing.

Vertellis is a European company concerned about the changes social media bring to connectedness. Their game moves players from small talk to genuine conversation. They believe that quality time offline coupled with a better understanding of oneself is crucial to coping with all this change in a healthy manner. It is their mission to make a positive impact in the world by facilitating meaningful conversations and giving people an outlet for self-reflection and development.

101 Conversation Starters for Families by Gary Chapman and Ramon Presson[4], is designed for families with children, but the questions will work for adults too. There is a Christian foundation to the book, and some items are drawn from examples in the Bible, but most are secular. Question 5: If you could be on any magazine cover, which one would you select? Question 15: Talk about a time when it felt good to help someone.

The Sunday Jar, or Conversation Jar, is a mason jar filled with insightful questions on strips of paper. Grab one, and you will have a conversation starter. I like this idea because you control the types of questions. These questions can be deep or focus on daily or weekly encounters. For example, "Who was the most interesting person you saw this week?"

Practice works.

Our family talks a lot. I've found that we learn more about each other than we knew before. The quality of sharing – these are interesting and meaningful comments made in passing – is much better. Change happens when you are aware of your interactions.

FOUR
WAYS TO PRACTICE BEING FRIENDS

A psychologist once shared a simple phrase with me, "We should treat family with the courtesy reserved for strangers." I tend to use little digs to make my point, not coming right out and saying what's bothering me. The pointed question: 'Are you actually done in here?'. The left-handed compliment: 'That would look great in warmer weather.' Or the old standard: 'Seriously?'

Rules of Engagement.

We all have baggage. Past wrongs, slights, feeling judged, or just the ways our personalities don't mesh (rubbing each other the wrong direction) create friction. We all have pressures. Maybe it's financial, health, or time demands. The goal is to carve out time when issues can be set aside so you can have a good time. We can do it, but it takes a concerted effort.

Limit Distractions.

Reduce distractions – silence your phone, tell the grandkids you'll be busy, and ignore your boss's texts. My husband calls it "never interrupt Charlie's Angels" time because when he was in high school, nothing came between that show and him.

Set Aside Topics.

Ban certain types of general discussions. Can't agree on politics? Let the political machine roll on for a few hours without you – unless you're a campaign manager and need to cry on a shoulder. Is Uncle Barry driving everyone crazy? Well, unless you need to come up with a plan to fix Barry, then set him aside.

I have a good friend, one of the kindest people I know, who complained about her daughter's housekeeping. Her daughter looked at her one day and said, "If you don't like it – leave." She stopped mentioning the housekeeping – in essence, accepting her daughter's differences as an adult.

Turn off the Complaint Machine.

No grousing about things that are out of our control, or that we are unwilling to change – a horrible boss, the cost of rent, or an unfinished project. Make the drama off-limits for a while. If nothing is going to change in a particular situation, there's no need to discuss it – focus on other more positive things.

Recognize and Acknowledge Everyone's Buttons.

If someone pushes your button, do not ignore it. Ask to change the topic. Try to be calm when you do it –explain that the subject bothers you (a bad haircut, bloating, a past boyfriend, the raise, etc.). Some issues fall into the 'agree to disagree' category. For Mom and me, one subject is national politics. We are both right in our own eyes, which is what happens when strong personalities come together.

Don't do the button-pushing. You know what I mean. If you start straightening up the minute you come through the door, and that makes your Generation Gal feel less than the beautiful and unique person she is, then don't do it. You would not straighten up your best friend's house unless both of you agreed to help each other with spring cleaning. Treat your intimate family friend in the same way.

Leave your sarcastic side in the car. Those little digs, while funny, can hurt others and yourself. Save those for when you need to slay the dragons – or deal with bad drivers.

Hit Reset.

Hit the reset button if things go badly during your friendship time. Do not leave thinking this friendship thing is not going to work – ask for a reset and begin again. For some of us, leaving baggage at the door takes practice, and we need to let our guard down so all of the good stuff can enter. It may not be perfect on the first day or some random day in the future. I'll twist a saying from a yoga instructor, 'Grace is like a blind date, and sometimes he just doesn't show up.' Sometimes we aren't in alignment, and it just doesn't work.

Just Say Yes – Be Curious – Be Kind.

Everyone needs to say yes to a new idea or agree to try something you haven't done for years. Try it at least once with the express purpose of hoping to catch the other person's enthusiasm. If you still don't like it, then you know this isn't an activity that you want to share. Caitlyn loves to go to thrift stores, and one of our creative activities upcycles thrift store finds. Mom went with us the first time and didn't enjoy herself as much as we did, and we didn't see the items we needed. She was recovering from a small knee injury on our next trip, so we sent photos of our finds while we were out. Yet once we completed the first upcycling challenge, Mom led the pack in hunting for thrift store items for the next challenge. I appreciate that she was an open and active participant – and the new ideas connected with her.

Everyone needs to ask questions and delve more deeply when a story is being told. Everyone needs to share. Everyone needs to play if there's a game. Just say yes, you never know what may happen in that hour or two.

Be very free with your sincere compliments, thank you, and WOW's – these multiply as you use them, so there is no need to be stingy. I tend to forget to articulate how amazing someone is, even though I'm thinking about it.

Tomorrow is soon enough to get back to the mundane parts of our lives. Suspend your reality...you may find that this new space becomes your new reality.

FIVE
FINDING TIME

Time fascinates me – I dwell on the concept. It is such a funny thing, either nothing is happening, or things are completely out of control. As a teenager, I was in a hurry. I finished high school in three years. I finished college in three and a half years. I always had places to go, things to do, people to see.

In my late twenties, I used to go to a tanning spa, the kind in the strip mall with the TAN sign above it. The place had these private rooms large enough to change clothes before sliding into the tanning coffin. I would lock that door, turn the music on my iPod up way too loud and slide into the tanning bed. I would lay there, knowing it was bad for my skin, but reveling in isolation. No one could call, no one could walk in, and no one could ask me for anything. Time was suspended for those 20 minutes while I would overheat, leaving my frustrations in the pool of sweat beneath my back.

I love to travel because I love new experiences. Each time I get on a plane to a new place, I wonder, "Will I remember this feeling of anticipation on my trip home? How can I capture the experiences, so they are fresh and new as memories?" I don't meditate, but for those moments before take-off, I would picture a Buddhist Monk reminding me to live in the moment.

Now that I'm older, my opportunities are changing. My children have children, and I'm not bound by constant practices, recitals, and homework schedules. So why does time slip away, into the ethos of engaging television, a good book, exercise routines, playing with fabric, or sleep?

Why am I not sending birthday cards and presents on the right dates…rather than randomly throughout the year? Why am I not calling my friends who are far away and having long chats? I'm not as good a friend at a distance. It has taken me a long time to accept that fact. I have to be asked to do things. I am not as good at initiating. I am best when joining activities that are in motion.

My work takes a lot of time and energy, plus I do have a husband, daughter, and grandson who want to see me. So, Mom and I get creative about finding time to hang out together and do new things. Our unwritten commitment is a few hours a week for new or outdoor activities. We do not have a Sunday family dinner ritual, but still, find ways to fit into each other's schedule consistently.

The Unusual Lunch Date.

Cross country skiing at lunch is one of my favorite activities. I work in a building that opens up to miles of groomed ski trails. We had a great time taking lessons at lunch for a month. There is something so fun about getting on our gear at noon for 90 minutes of skiing. It only happens once or twice a week, because we are so busy with other activities, but when it works, it's great.

During the summer, we try to walk at lunch a couple of days a week. The goal isn't to drive 30 minutes across town for a short walk; it is to fit an unexpected interaction into your daily routine. For us, it's hit and miss depending on Mom's commitments, so it's something we keep in mind without setting the appointments in stone.

Leaving Work Early.

We attend a yoga class for seniors, I'm just old enough to be eligible, and Mom is the oldest in the class. The drop-in class is late afternoon, so I sneak out of work early so we can join. Yoga is excellent because everyone works out at their level.

After Work Wind Down.

Osher Life Long Learning Center holds classes and hosts trips for adults who are 55 and older. Mom took a wine tasting course because I love wine, and she wanted to know more about the choices we were making. The course was four weeks from 3:30 PM – 4:45 PM at a nice restaurant in town. My Step-father dropped her off and I would meet her about the time class was ending.

We would order an appetizer. Mom would act as sommelier, telling me about the wines and why she scored them the way she did. Then she would select two different styles of wine for us to taste. For an hour, we would discuss wine, unwind, and explore new food. There was something about these interactions that was special. I don't know if it was because they were so relaxed or that they didn't require a substantial time commitment. We were extending our friendship by exploring something new.

Making Time Together Productive for Your Health.

I don't know anyone who doesn't get overscheduled or feel that they are letting down a special person sometimes. However, finding time to connect in ways that are active for your mind or your body does so much more than only sharing stories at dinner, it helps all of our generations' age more healthily.

SIX
BEING SOCIAL WITH FAMILY
MAKES US BOLDER

I asked, "Doing some research?" grabbing my first cup of coffee for the weekend.

"I'm looking for information on early-onset dementia." Mom had retired for the third time about a year before and just celebrated her 80th birthday.

"Interesting. Do you know someone who has dementia?"

"I think I may have it. I want to understand the symptoms so I can tell if it's coming on," Mom said. Her gaze was so intense when she looked up at me, that I didn't dare let out the bark of laughter I thought was appropriate. "I'm losing the power of language. I can't complete a sentence without having to hunt for a word or two somewhere in my grey matter. We're not talking about names or locations; these are just your common words we use every day."

All I know about dementia or Alzheimer's is that Ronald Regan and Margaret Thatcher both suffered. If the leaders of the Free World can have this condition, anyone can – including my mother. "And what have you found? Is there a correlation to losing speech?" I often wish my empathetic side jumped out in situations of stress or uncertainty as it does for my step-daughter and sister-in-law, who are nurses. They would be more understanding and less demanding.

"I'm still looking into it. I need to know," Mom says.

I left her to her research. How many times do we want a root cause for illnesses? Mentally, I begin listing environmental toxins and discard them out just as quickly: BPA, but she rarely drinks bottled water or soda; mercury, but we don't eat that much fish. As my list goes on, I realize she is old enough not to have been exposed to many of the modern toxins we fear today, and she would already be dead if the problem were unlined tin cans or unpasteurized milk. I walk away, knowing that she'll take care of everything first and then tell me what happened afterward.

__Lois:__ I read a lot, do puzzles, and get out to exercise. After my last retirement, I was spending a lot of time recovering from the exhaustion of bringing up a multi-million-dollar accounting system. Like many of us, I went from working way too many hours under a lot of stress to doing very little. My body needed a break, and I was more than willing to slow way down and enjoy sunrises and sunsets off our back deck.

After about six months, I noticed that the words I wanted to use were not immediately available; I had to go hunting for them. It didn't make sense to me — how could you lose the ability to do something you had done all your life. My experience wasn't the same as putting down my keys and forgetting where I left them; this was much more difficult.

Fairbanks has a learning center for seniors attached to the university. It is short classes taught by other seniors who have expertise or a passion for a subject. The program is robust and includes day trips, as well as international excursions to places like the Nile River or the Amazon. I signed up to go on a trip to the Arctic Circle. Fairbanks is about 200 miles south of the line on the map demarking the Arctic Circle around the top of the globe. I've wanted to go, but my husband wasn't interested, so this seemed like the perfect opportunity to see a part of Alaska I haven't seen and to meet some new people.

The trip was wonderful. Eight of us in a van, chatting, taking pictures, climbing around the rock formations, interacting. I signed up for more classes, some good, some not so good - but my hiatus at home was over.

And guess what. All those words I couldn't find suddenly became available on demand. It was a case of use it or lose it. Once I started engaging in a broader range of topics, my vocabulary came right back to me.

Getting Social, What the Research Tells Us.

Researchers in the late 1980's found that "social interaction has as much impact on physical health as blood pressure, smoking, physical activity, and obesity," according to as aging.org.

Medical News Today has an excellent article, 'What are the health benefits of being social?'[5] Psychologist Susan Pinker suggests that face-to-face contact is like a vaccine. Pinker explains that communication releases a cascade of neurotransmitters that protect you now and into the future lowering cortisol levels and stress. In the same article, they reiterate that social contact helps improve memory formation and recall while protecting the brain from neurodegenerative diseases. The Cognitive Neurology and Alzheimer's Disease Center at Northwestern University Feinberg School of Medicine found that SuperAgers defined as people 80 and above who have the mental agility of someone much younger appear to have one thing in common: close friends. This study looked at global areas, called Blue Zones, which have high concentrations of SuperAgers and found that while diet and lifestyle varied widely, all were very socially active. These individuals were surrounded by family and friends who actively support each other.

Friends Make Us Braver – Parents Embarrass Us.

Isn't it funny how we think of a friend's bold move as audacious or risk-taking? But if a parent or a child does something similar – or maybe even braver – we label them as crazy, embarrassing, looney, or socially inept. I believe, as teenagers, our friends had more comfortable relationships with our parents than we did. When the person's action doesn't reflect directly on us, as it does with relatives, we can watch in awe.

When I was 8 or 9, I loved my best friend's mother. She was young, hip, beautiful, and she had a cool name that I can't exactly remember, but I think it was Kiki, and she would say, 'Just call me Kiki.' Kiki knew the words to every – and I do mean every – song on the radio. We would test her, changing the station to find a song she didn't know. If I were to represent Kiki and me in a comic strip, she would have a golden glow surrounding her, and I would be staring with a heart beating out of my chest. I wanted to be just like her, and I still work to learn the words to every song on the radio!

My best friend, on the other hand, loved her Mom but was embarrassed by her mother's singing with the radio. She didn't appreciate Kiki's hip fashion and, in contrast, dressed very conservatively – or as conservatively as a nine-year-old can dress. My point is that she was embarrassed because Kiki's actions reflected on her, and they did not fit her perception of mother behavior.

We are not best friends with our parents at the age of 9. But as adults, the childhood perception that when you share blood, one person's actions reflect directly on you remains. This emotion is true for siblings, parents, grandparents, great grandparents. Friends are different, you can have a crazy friend or a bold friend or a flighty friend, and within reason, you do not feel their actions reflect directly on you.

What if we could put away the reflective mirror when we're out with our parent or our adult child? What if we could take advantage of their audaciousness and revel in their quirky side? We are not talking lousy behavior here, just those actions that we would enjoy – if only it weren't our mother, father, daughter, son, sister, brother – you get the idea. I found when I did that; I opened myself up to so much more joy.

The day was perfect for a beer, seventy-five degrees with clear skies. All of Fairbanks agreed with us and decided at 2:00 to checkout HooDoo, a new micro-brewery in town. HooDoo has no restaurant, only a counter to order beer with a limited seating indoors and a courtyard to enjoy. This was our first trip to the brewery.

The line to order and pick-up beer ran the length of the brewery's indoor seating, onto the steps to the courtyard, and about one-third of the way into the patio itself — a long line.

I immediately head to the windows to see exactly how far the line is snaking out the door – so we can decide whether to stay or go. I turn to ask Mom if she thinks it's worth waiting, and there she is standing in line. She's inserted herself in front of a thirty-something guy, who clearly knows better than to tell a little old lady she's cutting. Actually, Mom's just over five feet tall, so I can't be sure he has noticed her presence.

The daughter in me is horrified; after all, she cut the line. I've never read the book 'All I Really Need to Know I Learned in Kindergarten,' but I am confident that it says something about never cutting the line.

"Longline," I say. I have sidled over a casually as I can, and am standing outside the line.

"I think the line starts at the door," she says to me. I raise an eyebrow indicating exactly how much I believe that statement. "I'm over 80. I don't have time to stand in that line, and who is going to ask me to move." I do not look at the guy behind us as I slide into the line.

Mom's logic is flawless. I put away the mirror – the one that reflects on me – and decided to thank my lucky stars that my friend is so audacious. I know we'll be halfway through our beers before the line cleared. Plus, beer tastes even better knowing we broke a small social nicety to get it.

Mom's never felt that anyone's actions reflect on her or embarrass her, but she told this funny story about my grandfather putting his best foot forward. I do believe that I would have felt a twinge of embarrassment and hopefully would have set it aside.

Lois: My dad lost his teeth early in life and never bothered to get dentures. My children probably don't remember a time when dad had teeth. When he was in his late 80's or early 90's, I was playing on a recreational women's softball team. He was a widower and loved to flirt with the women on the team. He was always a favorite because he was gregarious and kind.

About halfway through the season, dad came out of the bedroom, ready to go to the game, and he looked different. He flashed me a winning a smile and said he was ready to go. He was wearing his brother's false teeth. I chuckled to myself because those teeth must have been so uncomfortable, but they made him feel so good.

Everyone still loved him and loved to flirt with him, and he felt terrific about himself. I never thought it reflected on me, but I did have to stifle a giggle the first few times I looked at him. I would think back to when I was young. Daddy explained that how you treat others is much more important than how you look, and his actions were often a reminder.

Hold your reaction long enough to evaluate the situation – letting go of your inhibitions can be liberating.

SEVEN
CHORES ARE ACTIVITY – GET YOUR FITBIT

Betty White is often asked how she stays so young and fit at 97. During Times Talk[6], she said, "I'm a health nut. My favorite food is hot dogs with French fries. And my exercise: I have a two-story house and a very bad memory, so I'm up and down those stairs."

Daily chores are activity, and while they might not be long enough or intense enough to replace a walk, yoga, or a trip to the gym, they are an essential part of keeping us moving. This concept seems so obvious, but my husband and my children were raised to do the heavy lifting. The men in my house carry the groceries, rearrange the furniture, unload the car, or take out the trash. I did these things when they weren't around, but if they were home, they took care of these chores. Okay, they don't necessarily scrub the bathtub or mop the floor, but they were taught to do the heavy lifting. "I'll carry that, Ma'am," my husband, Brent, tells Mom every time she gets home with a Cosco box full of groceries.

"I've got it," Mom says every time. Both are right. It's so nice to have a gentleman assist us with things that are heavy or awkward, but it's also better for us if we 'carry our own groceries.'

We need to change the terminology from "let me carry all of that for you" to "let me take some of the load." As we age, we need to carry our part of the load, because it keeps us healthy and robust.

Sharing of Talents Along with the Chores – Spring Cleaning.
My mother could be a professional organizer. I joke that she has hoarder

tendencies but is so good at finding places for everything that no one would ever know. I was talking about needing a case for my new ultrathin laptop, and she said, "I have a few laptop cases downstairs, let's see if we can find one that fits." She took me to a stack of eight cases neatly stowed on their shelf and found something that works. If a room starts bulging with 'stuff,' she buys something organizational and puts everything away.

When my house was full of kids, and I was traveling for work, things got chaotic and disorganized – okay – that is the case even now that the kids are grown and gone. My Mom sweeps in and gets me back to normal without throwing away anything. She says upfront, "you may have to hunt for something because my organizational thinking is different than yours, but it's here." I know how to organize, but it's in her DNA.

My daughter can scrub a room to within an inch of its life. When she attacks with a sponge and a mop, you know the corners are going to be clean. She likes to swipe and wipe. Unlike Mom and I, clutter doesn't bother her; she insists that her mind is so messy the room looks normal.

My talent is letting things go out of the door. For example, when I find I only have four knives and five salad forks, I buy a new set of silverware, so I have eight of everything. The old set immediately goes to the thrift store, not to the box of misfit utensils in the storage closet. I love to get rid of things, and sometimes I feel guilty about my desire to throw away items rather than just not buying them in the first place.

When my mother, my daughter, and I coordinate our talents and take on chores together, each bringing our expertise, we can get a lot done. We are each doing what we can, at the pace we can, and sharing in the experience. We are all lifting, shifting, and carrying as we spring clean and take stock. No one sits on the sidelines and directs, everyone does what they can, and we carry heavy boxes together. Yes, we're all a little stiff the next day, but no pain, no gain.

Alaska – Big State Means Big Chores.

In Alaska, the big chores come in fall and spring. Each fall, Mom and her husband, George, put up six to eight cords of wood. They say firewood keeps you warm twice – once when you cut it and once when you burn it. One cord is four feet high, four feet wide, and eight feet long (4x4x8). Cutting, splitting, and stacking eight cords takes 8 to 12 hours, and we try to finish during the weekend. (Last year, my husband and I cleared the land for our house, so we put up almost sixteen cords.) Everyone works. In the end, it is as if we have a one-story suburban home sided in small logs.

No one wants to go to the outbuildings that house the woodpile when it is 20 degrees below zero, so we store enough wood for a week or two in the garage.

On a warm winter day (anything above minus 10 degrees), moving wood from the stacks to the garage is a priority. Mom and I can do this quickly. Working together, we load a sled, and one pulls while the other pushes up the slight incline to the house. The person pushing also retrieves any dropped logs; we quickly stack and head back for another load.

"I thought of us during my storytelling class today," Mom said one night while we were stretching. "This woman told a story about her first year in Fairbanks."

The storyteller was new to Alaska. In the dead of winter, her heater stopped working, and they ran out of wood for the stove. The only option was to go to Spenards, a local lumber store, and ask about firewood. The guy behind the counter directed them to the lumberyard and explained wood was sold by the truckload. The evening was dark and freezing; the pile of wood was about ten feet tall. The woman telling the story said she climbed a little way up and tried grabbing a piece of wood, which was frozen to the pile. Using a pickaxe, she poked, prodded, and smacked the pile – working hard for every precious wood chunk. Another truck drove up. A small woman jumped out and clambered up the pile with her ax. She moved like a mountain sheep and chipped away at the ice, throwing piece after piece into the truck. She filled that truck so fast it made the storyteller's head spin. The woman had the body of a young girl, but the face of an older woman. When the newcomers finally filled their truck, they asked the man behind the counter about the woman. He said she was 90 years old and had been jumping up that woodpile weekly for as long as he could remember.

You Want Me to Do What?

I debated whether to write about things that should be labeled "Do Not Try This at Home" because social media comments can be judgmental. But if I'm trying to tell the story of two women aging as friends and family – then leaving out the activities deemed crazy by many would be disingenuous. And I hope we are still doing this together when she's 100 years old.

The house has a pitched tin roof that sheds snow. The large woodshop roof is not slanted enough to drop the snow's accumulation. Late each winter, we extend our very long ladder the 20 feet to reach the roof. Anyone living in a snowy climate has most likely seen people removing snow from a flat-roofed commercial building or garage.

The good news is that the roof is tin, so large chunks of snow cut from the snow block covering the roof can be pushed off the edge rather than lifted and thrown. The bad news is, as the snow disappears, the roof begins to resemble an ice rink that was just smoothed by a Zamboni.

When the temperature reaches the upper teens or 20's, it is warm enough that we can shed our jackets after working up a sweat without freezing the small hairs on our faces. Chopping free and sliding a three-foot snow-berg is hard work. It requires too much oxygen to breathe through a scarf so our faces must be exposed.

I hold the twenty-foot ladder for Mom as she climbs up with her plastic wide-mouthed shovel. She returns the favor, holding the ladder from the roof. Planting our feet in the roof's snow, which can be anywhere from just above the knees to our waists, we survey the three-car garage sized area.

Snow is removed by driving the shovel straight down and then pushing the chuck of snow off the edge. The beauty of Fairbanks during the winter is that it stays cold and has low humidity. The snow may be deep, but it remains light and fluffy throughout the winter. There are no snowmen in front yards because the snow doesn't stick together well enough to create two giant balls of ice.

Half of your shoveling time is spent pushing snow uphill, while the other half is pushing downhill. You would think the downhill pitch would be easier, but it is more challenging. The roof is slick, remember the Zamboni, and you have to walk up the slope to get the next scoop of snow. The screws holding the tin on the roof down make shoveling a bear, but they also hold your boots in place as you move around the roof. This year, something must have shifted because there were so few screws that Mom and I looked like a repeating loop from America's funniest home video – fall, struggle to get upright, move snow, fall, struggle to get upright, move snow – repeat. We were far enough from the edge that I wasn't worried about us pitching over the backside, but much of our energy was spent just returning to the upright position.

At one point, my shovel went flying off with what I believe was a world record-sized snow-berg. "Well, you have to go get it," said my mother. I was considering jumping off the roof into the snowbank, but then Mom said, "I'll hold the ladder," and I came to my senses. Getting to the ladder required a logistics plan that would have made an Arctic explorer proud.

"You have to get to my center pile of snow first," I said. We are great at stating the obvious. There are eight feet between where Mom stood and the center rectangle of snow.

"I realize that," she acknowledges and begins sliding her feet along the roof. "I'm feeling for screws," she explains. She finds a screw and begins the sliding movement with her other foot. It was skating in slow motion. One foot is sliding gracefully along the roof as the other remains planted on the nail. The skating show ends at my rectangle of snow, and both of us begin high stepping toward the ladder.

After I've trudged through the waist-high snow behind the building to recover my scoop, she catches me. "Why don't you bring up the big blue shovel?" she says. It's the type with the double-sized bucket, and a metal handle long enough for two people. "I like that one, and it will make this go much faster."

"You think?" I ask, remembering the feel of my shovel pitching off the roof and think this shovel is destined for the back-snow bank. My mother is audacious, but she's also cautious – in many ways, more careful than I am – so I know she won't be pitching off the roof. I put my head through the handle holding the shovel sideways on my shoulders, put my wrist through my shovel and started to climb. "Next year, we're hiring Sherpas," I tell her. "I don't mind the work, but lugging the gear is a drag."

Watching her slide around with that giant shovel, which was effective in her capable hands, entertained me for the rest of the project. I'm confident she felt the same about watching me fall out of the snow rectangle, slide my snow-bergs off the pitch, and carefully find my way back to the security of the snow pile.

"The guys would say they could do this faster," I said. "They complain when we come up."

"Do we need it done faster?" she asks as we stand on the clear roof sipping coffee and Bailey's provided by her husband. She should get an honorary doctorate from Harvard because she always knows the right question to ask. Speed wasn't important; working hard, working together, and doing something meaningful was what counted.

EIGHT
EXERCISE TOGETHER

The journey to consciously improve all of our lives began with a set of hand weights and a video. We have always been active, some would say inspirationally active, but once Mom hit her eighties, I felt I needed to work out without Mom, using walks, rides, or skiing with her as a supplement to my workouts. A British arms fitness video and two sets of hand weights changed all of my preconceived notions – almost overnight.

Mom came back, a little more than a year ago, from renovating one of their rental properties in Colorado fifteen pounds lighter and feeling good. She radiated good health. Their Spartan diet of sandwiches reduced the number of calories, and their tight renovation schedule kept them physically active from morning until evening.

On one of our hikes, we decided it was time to get in shape for summer, and our problem area was the upper arm – fondly referred to as bat wings. A blogger linked us to a 20-minute arms workout where an adorable British trainer taught ten exercises. She started with three-pound weights. In the first two weeks, we spent most of our time rewinding the video to see which movement was next in line – you would think with only ten, we could keep the order straight. My mother, ever-efficient, created a list of the moves, and the routine started going faster. We moved to five-pound and then to eight-pound weights within a few weeks.

We kept thanking each other for being an exercise partner. Weight lifting, going to the gym, or other organized exercise is tough to do without a partner – it's too easy to put it off to the next day. People who exercise with partners improve because they are consistent.

Mom pulled out articles and books on exercises for those who are aging, and we built those into our routine. The arm exercise moved from 20 minutes to 45 minutes with stretching on the floor and leg work. Then we added a few balance exercises. When we do the full routine, it takes about 50 minutes. I realized in these sessions that weights are perfect because we can each use different sized weights to meet our specific needs.

My grandson was two when we started and joins in with his set of one-pound weights. He learned to count to fifteen coaching us through all of our repetitions. We are his jungle gym – he crawls under us as we were doing planks, an exercise where only your elbows and your toes touch the floor, so you look like a tabletop. He was slightly injured twice, walking into our moving weights, now he's more cautious.

Besides realizing there are exercise routines that allow each person to move at their own pace, I was surprised at how quickly Mom improved. I keep harping about preconceived notions of aging. Her balance, flexibility, strength, and stamina improved at the same rate as mine. Exercising at any age will produce positive results.

My sister, Linda, is fifteen years older than I am, and she used to joke with me, "As you age, you realize those ancient people aren't that ancient after all." Mom may be almost ninety, but she is more than able to determine how far to push her body without getting injured while getting maximum gain from working out.

As we added to our routine, I started looking for exercises that allowed each person to progress at a different pace, and we began to explore organized activities more closely.

Mind to Muscle.

"There's a four-week mobility class for seniors I'm going to check out," Mom said. "Maybe we will get some new moves" This part of our general plan to bring home new ideas or information if we couldn't attend together. Her experience is pretty funny.

Lois: This was a class of active seniors; everyone looked active and must have cared about exercise because we all had mid-range tennis shoes and reasonable athletic wear. The instructor has us lay down and explained that we were going to get in touch with our muscles, really in touch with how they felt and how they moved.

We laid there for an hour, slowly lifting a leg – at a glacial pace – and evaluating the feel of the movement. About half-way through I wanted to scream, I had never moved so slowly in my life, and I had just gone through physical therapy for a hip replacement! He would murmur in a relaxing tone, so I couldn't hear what he was saying.

I kept going back thinking there might be an epiphany in the next hour, plus I had a drawing course immediately after the session ended. The class got smaller and smaller. You have to try new things because something might change your life. This class was not one of those things.

The ironic part is that I have a kink in my neck. I'm convinced it came from working so hard to move so slowly in that class.

Yoga.

The participant can individualize yoga. It stresses balance, something that is very important as we age. Everyone in a yoga class goes at their own pace by modifying the moves to fit their needs. We have many books on yoga, and I loved doing yoga with a video from Rachel Welch many years ago, so we added various moves to our nightly arm routine.

I took a five-week class to learn how to improve our posture and expand the number of moves we could do at home. Mom and I then took an organized class so she could have the yogi adjust her positions. I loved the course because it put Mom and me at the same level of knowledge — we each became responsible for our body positions.

Early in our yoga training, I traveled for a week. We texted each other when we had finished the sun salutations to support our continued exercise.

My favorite part about yoga is the attitude of the instructors; they begin by telling us, "You are here today for you, and your body is your guide. The goal is a strain, not pain." The variations for each movement and accessories allow everyone to participate in every move.

Mom's favorite yoga-like move at home is lying on her stomach, reaching her arms as far in front of her head as she can. She says it makes her taller. Some of our best conversations begin when we're holding a stretching move — we get distracted, sit on the floor, and talk — then we move on to the next position. It isn't disciplined, but it gets the job done.

My nieces in Virginia attend yoga classes, and Mom can go and feel comfortable doing something active with them that everyone will enjoy. She joined my brother and nephew at hot yoga. She said exercising at 100+ degrees made you sweat. She was tired at the end and would love to do it again.

Cross Country Skiing.

Taking cross country skiing lessons during lunch was a dream come true. Unlike exercise with a mirror, in skiing, you rely on someone else to watch you and give feedback. I wish we had taken a class ten years earlier.

We needed to set the expectations with the other participants. I was the youngest, at 55, and Mom was the oldest at 87. Most of the participants were in their mid-sixties to early seventies. The few times Mom fell, they would all turn to me, waiting for me to go and help her up. I explained that we were in the ski class because we are both physically able to ski, which includes getting up after a fall. Even after my explanation, the male students would still go to help her up. Being helped up after falling on cross country skis is an excellent thought - but it does not make any sense – another skier grabbing you is not helpful. I chuckled as each nice gentleman would come over to me and say, "She says she can do it herself." She can. And those gentlemen could also get up after a fall. Everyone ages differently, so you can't make assumptions based solely on age. You have to trust that each person in the class is physically able to participate.

Mom did twist a knee on the second-to-last lesson and decided to rest it rather than attend the last class. It healed, and we were back out in a few weeks.

Community 5K or 10K.

You are never too old to train for a walking/racing event. In Fairbanks, the longest day of the year, which features more than 23 hours of sunlight, is celebrated with a community 10K race. The race is competitive and social, with elite athletes competing for the best time, and mothers pushing strollers just participating. Since her late 70's, Mom has won her age category. When she turned 80, she was the fastest in her age group and the 75-80-year-olds. The first year I moved here, we completed the race together when Mom was in her late 70's. We crossed the finish line, and she had to sit down. Her legs were cramping, and her back was killing her. "Well, this was a bad idea," was my reaction. "We'll do other things, but never do this again." Mom decided she needed to be in better shape for the next race, so we started walking with determination.

The next week, we began walking three miles – a mile and a half downhill and a mile and a half uphill – near the house. When we started after that first race, we took a full bottle of water with us, and we had to stop at least four times on the way home. Now we take a half bottle of water and stop once or twice. We are in better shape. We talk almost all the way. We are not pushing our heart rates to the top of any range; we are just consistently exercising and enjoying the benefits.

Last year, at 87, she won her age category with her new hip. We decided before the race not to kill ourselves to finish - it was a no strained muscle zone. We were about 8 minutes slower than the previous year's competition because we took time to sip 3 ounces of beer, high five a dinosaur, and take a photo of one of the most specular sunsets in Fairbanks. Each year we have gotten stronger and faster. We stay ahead of muscle deterioration through exercise.

Mom's new goal is to walk the course of a difficult 26-mile marathon here in town. Not to compete the day of the marathon, but to try it on a cool day. We'll take a backpack with drinks and maybe lunch. The goal is to experience a marathon with hills and complete it – not for a medal, but ourselves.

From our teens to our sixties, we train harder if we are not achieving our goals. So why did I think that we should never do the 10K again because Mom's legs and back were hurting? I needed to stop using age as a yardstick for activity – if training more intensely works for a sixty-year-old, then, of course, it will work for an eighty-year-old. Everyone benefits from physical activity as long as they understand their limits as they train.

Tai Chi.

I want to try Tai Chi with Mom. I have only done it a few times and love the graceful movements. I appreciate that it can be done anywhere at any time. This type of exercise connects you with nature and your body. Once you learn a few patterns, you can repeat them again and again. It builds strength and balance – two things we need as we age.

Jazzercise/Zumba.

Jazzercise is another exercise model where the moves can be modified based on your fitness level. While Mom has never attended, the classes I have and enjoy the music and laidback attitude. The old aerobics classes I loved in college have morphed into Zumba and Jazzercise. Both are good for the body and good for the spirit.

Dance.

I married my husband because he could dance. We spent years turning heads at every country bar with a dance floor. Many hours were spent line dancing with my girlfriend. She would write the steps so we could practice in the living room. When my daughter said she wanted to learn to two-step, swing, and line dance and that she wanted me to go with her – I wanted to jump up and down. Of course, I want to go and to practice in the kitchen anytime. To me, this is the adult version of playing catch with your kid – and there's music!

Make It Work.

Get creative about making exercise work. I started training to run a race with my cousin. Mom meets me at the bottom of the hill for the one-and-a-half-mile walk home. She delays her start by 15-20 minutes so I can run three miles before meeting her.

We struggle at the beginning of any new activity. At the end of the first session with the three-pound weights, we could not lift our arms above our heads. Now we can shake our weights over our heads to celebrate another activity that keeps us living longer, healthier lives.

NINE
OUTDOOR ACTIVITIES
PUTTING FEAR IN ITS PLACE

Self-preservation is one of our strongest instincts. For decades, experts who study needs, put health, safety, and security at the top of the list. Advertisers want to see us use the tools to live safer, more productive, more independent lives. Ads for home security systems, smoke detectors, insurance, and LifeLine monitoring devices remind us nightly about the perils of living, especially as we age. Add to this list the length of time it takes to recover from an injury, and it may seem like the couch is the safest place.

I believe our fear is about the unknown. 'I don't know if you can do this activity' meets 'I don't know if I can cope emotionally if something bad happens' in the worst possible combination. It makes us overprotective, nervous, and wishing we had just gone out to lunch!

I find the fear blindsides me – always catching me off-guard. My heart starts to beat faster. I feel an overwhelming sense of responsibility. Here's the reality, I live with an 87-year-old woman who skis, hikes, bikes, shovels the roof, and understands her limitations. I am physically able to do anything I darn-well, please. I am never concerned when we start an activity; the overwhelming responsibility hits me while we are in the middle of the action. A trip – not even a fall - on gravel or ice – sometimes drives me to want to move over and hold my mother's elbow. And yes, first cross country skiing fall of the season is harsh – fear grabs me by the throat.

How do you let this fear go – not bury it away for later – but let it go? I remind myself, "We are both adults and able to articulate what we need."

Sometimes I only have to tell myself once, and my fears disappear. Sometimes I have to repeat this again and again – like a mantra. I dissect what is bothering me about the situation and decide if a small adjustment will make me more comfortable.

Small Adjustments Make a Big Difference.

Last winter, we were walking down the road, which in Alaska, that generally means walking under the light of the moon or with a flashlight. I wasn't wearing my glasses, and we didn't take a torch. I was unable to distinguish the ditch from the road. It was slick in the middle of the road, so we were walking along the side, and I was terrified Mom would fall in the ditch and hurt her new hip. I couldn't get it out of my mind, so we discussed my fears. Mom had her glasses on and reassured me that everything looked fine. My brain refused to trust her enough to let the fear go. I know my mother will always keep us safe, but now I take my glasses, so I never have to experience unnecessary anxiety like that again.

Releasing Responsibility Back to the Right Person.

If I need help, I ask. If Mom or Caitlyn need help, they ask. I release responsibility for my mother and daughter back to them – I am not their keepers. I am their friend. I trust them to make decisions about activities for themselves. If you can allow your companion to be responsible or herself or himself, then a small stumble stays where it needs to – locked in that moment. You are giving yourself the freedom to enjoy the rest of the trip.

My yoga instructors remind me to make modifications to the movements, so they <u>fit where you are today</u>.

Physical health improves when we are consistently moving; mental outlook improves when we are getting better at that movement. Don't let fear stop you from being active together. Are you feeling a little under the weather? You can still get moving. If you are completely wiped out from a hectic day – say so – and take the day off.

There is a crazy race called the Eco-Challenge (www.ecochallenge.com). Teams of four race non-stop across hundreds of miles of mountains, jungles, or oceans. The first team to cross the finish line with all four members win. If a team loses a member, they are out of the race. Each team must have at least one person of the opposite sex. Teams that complete the challenge understand the importance of honest communication because it serves them so well in this stressful situation. Ian Adamson, one of the most successful adventure racers in the world, talks about simple check-ins, such as, 'How's everyone feeling?' or 'Is the pace okay?' and how every racer is responsible for answering honestly.

Conversations about Getting Active.

These are a few maxims we use when we are active. The 'I' could be either Mom or me on any given day.

Statement	Response
I will invite you because we are more likely to be active together.	I will let be honest if I'm not feeling up to accepting your invitation.
Situation: Mom and I are more consistent with our arm exercises when we do them together. We are direct in asking, "Do you want to do arms tonight?" rather than assuming we know the answer.	
If I don't feel physically able to do something, I will tell you. And I will let you know when I feel ready to do something more difficult.	I will adjust what we are doing to meet your needs, making certain that my needs are met as well.
Situation: Some weight exercises flare up my tendinitis. I do the exercises without weights and marvel at why they don't hurt Mom.	
I will let you know if I need help, and I will let you how to help me.	I will listen and do as you ask.
Situation: The hill is too steep to climb unassisted. "Stand here so I can push on your shoulder to get up this hill." One of us has stepped off the trail and sunk in deep snow. "Put your hand out so I can use it to leverage myself up, but don't pull."	
I will let you know when I'm uncomfortable, not so we can go home, but so we can adjust what we're doing.	I will brainstorm how to make us more comfortable, but will not insist on driving you home.
Situation: Taking photos when the temperature is below. We now keep chemical hand warmers in our gloves and pockets.	

Statement	Response
I will encourage you to be the best you can, including suggesting that we finish the activity, but will respect you if you've had enough.	I will go farther if I can because I want to feel that sense of achievement.
Situation: I say, "We've done two of the three hills; do you think that's enough?" Mom says, "It's not that much further if you want to keep going."	
I will encourage you to go at your pace.	I will wait for you ahead.
Situation: Climbing the hill sections of the trail. No one should ever be left behind! We use this technique for short uphill stretches on familiar trails.	

We also have a series of one-sided pledges.

One-Sided Pledges
I will set aside my fears and focus on us.
I will do my best, and you will do your best, so we are both getting the most we can out of the adventure.
I will not hover over you.
I will share information about my aches and pains with you.
I will laugh.
If I accidentally put a fish hook in your arm, I will help get it out.

Riding a Bike – Something You Never Forget.

Riding a bike is a procedural memory, which is a type of long-term memory that lets your body remember how to do certain things. When my mother mentioned hopping on her bike again, after a five-year hiatus, I paused for a second – but only a second – after all riding a bike is something you never forget.

Lois: I enjoyed biking, and once Cathy returned to Fairbanks, it was time to start again. You go further than you do when you're walking. I had to work to get my leg over the center bar, and there were a few false starts as I remembered how to change gears. I could see Cathy cringe the first time I hopped off. She has had many more injuries than I have over the years, and I think she was projecting her fears onto me.

In the end, she held the back of the seat so I could take off. And once I was going, I felt great. Stopping was another matter. My body knew what to do, but my mind kept telling me I couldn't. I would slam on the brakes, which threw the bike out of balance. I needed to tame my doubt and not overreact.

We practiced by the house until I felt confident. The next day we went to a bike trail in town. I was again slamming on the brakes. It was strange not to be able to control how my body reacted to my unconscious fear. Still, I knew it was just fear. Then everything clicked; my body found the rhythm, and my mind allowed me to glide to a stop – rather than clutching the breaks. Cathy had a big smile when we dismounted, telling me that she imagined catastrophe at the intersection ahead.

After a few shaky starts and stops, I was back to my old self, flying down the road and enjoying the scenery. Biking is one of those activities where people looked shocked when I climb off my bike and remove my helmet. That reaction gives me a little zing.

We both knew I could bike. It was so lovely going with someone that helped me be successful rather than spending the whole time telling me to be careful. I know my limitations – I don't need someone else telling me what they believe.

Here's what Mom does not know. My husband bought her a new mountain bike with a girl's crossbar, so it is much lower. She will be able to get on and off with ease. She could keep riding her current bike, but it does not fit her as it should. I can't wait until next summer!

TEN
WHEN YOU ARE REALLY SCARED
THINK OF US

Most of our family lives in Colorado, so you would think Mom and I would be in the state at the same time, but that rarely happens. On one such occasion, we decided to take a hike with my best friend in the foothills outside Boulder. Boulder is a mile (5,280 feet) above sea-level, while Fairbanks is 446 feet above sea-level, so it can take a couple of days to acclimate to the lower oxygen levels.

The day after we arrived, Mom, Evie, and I hiked a series of beautiful ridgelines where the trail is like narrow steps up the side of the rock. The views were spectacular, and the climb was just challenging enough. The day was beautiful in the shade and hotter than heck in the sun, typical Boulder weather. As we worked our way along the mountain, there would be a steeper uphill section, then a flat section, repeating several times.

At one point, Mom said she felt a little dizzy, so we sat on a rock in the shade and had some water. She felt better, so we continued the upward trek, again she said she felt dizzy, and we stopped for shade and water. By this time, I'm getting concerned. I begin to use all of my problem-solving skills in this situation. Can we go back? No, that's impractical because it's too narrow, and others are coming up. Is it closer to go back? Notice I don't care that it is unrealistic, I just want to know the shortest way off of the mountain. I blamed myself. We should have waited another day to hike. We should have never hiked. Why did we leave Alaska? Why didn't I put the phone number for search and rescue in my cell?

I become irrational. I am stealing everyone's responsibility, not because Evie and Mom are unable to make decisions for themselves, but because I am so overcome with guilt about the situation. And here's the case, we are on a hike. It is hot. Mom's feeling dizzy. This is my first experience with the guilt and fear we experience once we notice our parents aging. Our instinct is to do ANYTHING to protect these folks because they suddenly seem mortal.

I love my best friend Evie, and she is a rock. While I keep asking silly questions, she drinks water with Mom and has a lovely conversation. She and Mom both know that we need to wait and hydrate so that the dizziness will pass. It's altitude sickness, and Mom isn't the only one on the mountain experiencing it. Evie's calm eventually envelopes me. Mom begins to feel better.

As she begins to feel like herself, I become jubilant —a weight has been lifted from my shoulders. I am floating as we head downhill. To this day, anytime I think about the last part of that journey makes me smile.

I often reflect on that hike as a reminder to be patient and trust those people around me. Remembering helps me put that fear in its place.

A Canoe Trip to Remember.

Lois: My father lived with my husband and me full-time for the last ten years of his life. Dad and my husband, George, were avid outdoorsmen who loved to hunt, fish, and camp. When dad was 88 or 89, we headed into the Alaska wilderness to hunt moose along with my brother-in-law, and a young nephew.

We camped along the river inlet about forty miles north of Fairbanks, Alaska. Fairbanks is in the center of Alaska, far from the ocean, in an area between two vast mountain ranges with smaller ranges nearby. The plan was to canoe in and out of the hunting grounds.

Early the first morning, we donned our life vests and slipped the first canoe into the water. The Cola-Cola logo emblazoned on the side made me smile. The day was dawning bright and clear with that crispness unique to the air in fall. I took the rear position, and daddy took the front. My husband, brother-in-law, and nephew would follow in the second canoe with the guns and gear. Unbeknownst to us, it had rained hard upriver overnight, creating less than favorable conditions for the float trip.

Twenty minutes in, I could feel the water tugging on our canoe, and I keep telling dad that we want to stay left near the shore. The two of us are paddling hard to maintain that position, but the current keeps pulling us back toward the center of the river. Suddenly I see the problem. A tree that has fallen and is hanging more than halfway across the water. The birch is full of autumn leaves. The branches are touching the river bottom, but the trunk is above the waterline. These trees are called sweepers because they sweep the water, and everything floating on the river, under the trunk.

There's always that moment when you know things are going to go horribly wrong. We are paddling hard, but the canoe heads right for the tree. Worse yet, the back of the boat begins to cantilevering around its front.

We flip the canoe and go under the tree. I hit the riverbed with my knees tucked and bounced right back up to the surface. I immediately look for the canoe and my dad. He is far in front of me, with an arm over the upside-down canoe, holding on and riding it down the river. I know the next canoe is coming, and I am in its path. My hands are tangled in the tree, allowing me to use the trunk to pull myself to shore.

The minute my feet touch the shore, I start running down the side of the river screaming 'HELP! HELP!' as loud as I can. I look back and see my husband's canoe go over, knowing they can't rescue dad, I keep running and screaming.

I am so lucky because ahead of me, there is a camp, and the guys are still there. When the man hears me scream, he jumps out of his tent, assesses the situation and heads straight for his canoe. He and daddy lodge the canoe on a sandbar, and then he pulls dad into his boat.

Onshore, Dad's shaking violently. We get him into a sleeping bag, wrap hot rocks from the fire in a towel, and put those in with him. He keeps saying he'll be fine if he can have a nip of brandy, but I'm an EMT and know you don't give alcohol to someone suffering from hypothermia. Eventually, I acquiesce, open the flask, and help him get it to his lips.

I am overwhelmed with guilt. All I can think about is how I will need to call my five brothers and sisters to explain that I killed daddy? My mind is reeling with recriminations about the choices I'd made, the kind of irresponsible daughter I am, and what my siblings are going to think about me.

Thank heavens I didn't need to make that call. Another hunter came upriver in a motorboat and carried us back to our camp with our canoes — but no gear — we left it at the bottom of the river to be rescued another day.

After a few days, daddy was back to normal and ready for the next adventure. It took me a while to get over the guilt and to stop wanting to tie him to the kitchen chair. He told the canoe story a thousand times over the next eight years, impressing his family and friends. And we kept going out for adventures until the day he passed away.

I was in my sixties when this happened. Age doesn't matter when you are dealing with your parents and their health. What is happening at that moment is all that matters. I'm so glad I didn't let this one incident keep us from hunting, fishing, and camping for the next eight years.

I remember the day Mom called to tell me my grandfather passed away. He was in his mid-90's. She said George, her husband, had taken granddad fishing. They caught their limit of salmon, stopped to look at the Denali peak shining in the sun on a beautiful day. On the trip, they saw wildlife and fantastic scenery. The doctor speculated that grandpa was so relaxed on the drive home that he slipped away in his sleep. While Mom was crying when she called to tell me, we both agreed that he lived a great life and passed after doing something he loved – does it get better than that?

Think of Us.

No matter how hard we try, there will be situations where we feel responsible for the distress of another. When that happens, I ask Mom to tell me about the most distressing moment with her dad, and I just let my worries float away.

ELEVEN
GETTING CREATIVE

Caitlyn isn't a fan of hiking, weights, or yoga, so when we talked about how to spend our time, she suggested focusing on creativity. We met at the kitchen table to lay out a plan. The first brainstorming session is where we determined the categories for this book: physical activities, creative activities, and sharing memories.

We planned for the next few months as if we were planning a vacation. We brainstormed about our interests and what we would like to discover. We have not done many things on our list, for example, a canoe trip down the Brooks Range or upcycling a piece of furniture. But our chances of doing these things is higher if we have them on the list.

Creative challenges allowed us to interact as friends — not just family - in a unique way. Art has fewer rules and no judgment. If you didn't like it, you ditched it. Conforming was not required. Each person's work was unique, and the pieces did not need to fit together. Assistance, not guidance, was appreciated. Suggestions were offered upon request.

We painted, decorated, and attended cultural events. Each season brought new events, and we worked to look at one recurring activity with fresh eyes. All outings and creative sessions ended with a small celebration. Rather than just parting ways, we wound down with cheese, crackers, and wine or a cozy coffee at our favorite restaurant. Positive closure was vital to us. Think of it as a date with your best friends and make it unique.

Benefits of Creativity as We Age.

Exercising the brain is as essential as exercising the body. I wanted to understand why I feel better when I'm pursuing a creative activity and how to boost the power of those positive experiences.

Many of the studies on creativity and aging point to art therapy, with the authors extrapolating their findings to older individuals.

The data is encouraging – all forms of creative endeavor benefit us as we age. In *The Benefits of Creativity for Older Adults*, Carleen Brice interviews Tim Carpenter, founder and executive director of EngAGE[7]. "Americans see getting older as this ending point and decline, whereas research on the brain shows the opposite. Your brain increases its ability to make new connections," says Carpenter. "Our brain continues to grow as we get older, and certain forms of creativity fire neurons in a way that creates connections in the brain."

The article 'Aging: What's Art Got To Do With It?' states that art enhances cognitive function[8]. The author Barbara Bagan, Ph.D., ATR-BC stresses that "the imagination and creativity of older adults can flourish later in life, helping them to realize unique, unlived potentials..." The article continues, "Making art or even viewing art causes the brain to continue to reshape, adapt, and restructure, thus expanding the potential to increase brain reserve capacity."

When viewing or creating art and music, our self-esteem increases. We become more playful (and who doesn't want that). We have spiritual connectedness, improved cognitive abilities, and a stronger sense of identity.

Music therapy is just beginning to deal with age-associated hearing loss. In noisy rooms, I cannot hear a single person speaking; however, I'm fine in a quiet place. Mom has trouble hearing directionally, so if I am behind her, she cannot understand me. In 2017, I listened to a National Public Radio (NPR) All Things Considered piece, " 'Like Brain Boot Camp': Using Music to Ease Hearing Loss" [9], about music therapy. Frank Russon, professor of psychology and director of the Science of Music, Auditory Research and Technology Lab at Ryerson University in Toronto, is working on this problem. Research shows that aging musicians fare better at distinguishing speech from noise than non-musicians. He is working with choir participants on locking into pitch when there is background music or sound. The article has clips so you can test your hearing. I am experimenting with music to help my hearing.

We all experience the benefit of creativity, no matter the generation.

Use Photography to Find a New World View.

In the basement of my office building hang black and white photos taken in the 1960s and 1970s of Native Alaskan village life. I'm drawn to these photos – their sense of community and fun. The tug-of-war on the tundra near the sea makes me giddy. Village elders look on as young boys and girls in their muck boots strain to take control of the rope. Their wrinkled faces show a love of the moment and reflect their remembrance of tugs-of-war from their childhoods. Another photo captures older women laughing with unabandoned joy; their eyes are slits behind their upturned cheeks. Theirs is the carefree laughter of friends and family who shared a lifetime of experiences, so they all understand the joke.

To capture moments that move people takes a photographer's artistic eye. That artist was trusted by the people and was unobtrusive so that natural expressions came to life.

I have repeatedly mentioned that my mother is an avid photographer specializing in landscapes and cityscapes. She wanted to try a series of new settings on her camera, so we headed up the trail behind the house. We walk this trail at least twice a week in all seasons – so we should know every inch by heart. On this trip, various stands of trees created abstract art as Mom set the camera for night mode and then moved it up and down, blurring the tree trunks. For another, broken stumps and flowers were captured with a blurred background to look more three-dimensional. This new focus – pun intended – changed how we experienced the trail. Between us, we have hundreds of photos on the path and yet this exercise gave us an entirely new perspective. It took something routine and made it fresh again.

Since that day, I've found new ways to enjoy the trail. On one outing with my grandson, we created dinosaur scenes in the undergrowth. The pictures make the small plants and dinosaurs look huge. I felt like a filmmaker, and he loves looking at his dinosaurs staring in this mini-photo grouping.

***Lois:** I sometimes wonder why I take photos of the same scenery year after year. I have my camera ready for each trip in and out of Alaska. I find it hard to pass this beautiful landscape without wanting to capture the moment for eternity. My mind tells me the scenery is different enough that it must be captured anew.*

Each winter, sections of Fairbanks look like something from a Hans Christian Andersen story. In the lower 48, frosted evergreens last a day or two after a big storm. Here, the cold temperatures combined with steam coming from the warm water near the power plant, create thirty-foot trees thick with white snow. Hoarfrost, which is fascinating microscopic drops of air that freeze against the snow, creates a frosty sheen.

My daughter and I wait until the temperature warms to just above zero. We move from location to location, capturing the stillness of winter and the movement of the steam swirling above the warm rushes of water. My fingers ache as the cold drives me back to the car's efficient heater every 30 minutes. Once I can feel my fingers, the pink glow of the sun beckons, and I pull back on my thin gloves. We finally give in to the cold when the sun is too low in the sky and head to a restaurant with a heated bar rail to drink a glass of wine.

I upgrade my photography equipment and take classes because I want to produce photography that has the technical clarity to rival the great professionals. It's something I will never stop working on perfecting – and I know each time I take photos of familiar territory, I am better prepared to capture scenery from new places I've never been.

Overcoming Artistic Shyness.

Art is a solitary pursuit for me. I have many pieces of work hidden in the bottom of a box to be "fixed" or "tossed" later. Learning a new technique in class is fun. Working on a blank canvas near others is scary. Besides, I am one of those annoying people who fill every silent moment with sound – talking, music, television.

Caitlyn is comfortable being creative around others – her style is free and easy. She loves bouncing ideas off others. Opinions are requested and promptly ignored if they don't fit her vision. She is a member of the YouTube generation, where people post fantastic fails.

Mom is quiet when creative. The rest of the world falls away as she concentrates on projects. Her style is technical. She can block out the noise and chaos. I have always wondered if growing up with five siblings gave Mom a lot of practice ignoring what was happening around her.

Caitlyn grabs a brush and goes for it, mom grabs a ruler and pencils to set an underlayment, and I sit and think. Doing art together is much more fun when you understand and appreciate each person's approach. They are concentrating on their work, not judging your process.

One of our first creative home nights followed the structure of Paint Nite, an event where people meet at a restaurant or bar to paint a canvas following an instructor's tutelage. The predetermined composition, instructions, and wine helped participants feel comfortable painting in a crowd. Participants paint in bursts: Quick instructions, turn up the music and brush for ten minutes, two minutes to chat with a neighbor, and the cycle begins again.

We found instructions on YouTube. Caitlyn, in her usual style, selected a different painting, choosing to march to the beat of her drummer. We started at 9:00 PM and went to bed at 1:00 AM. The hours between included constantly rewinding the video to hear the instructions, music, laughing, and wine.

We've grown artistically since that first evening. Now each person selects a photo or a picture to paint: no instructor and nothing predetermined. As usual, Caitlyn operated outside the box choosing a funky wooden camper trailer birdhouse as her canvas.

I selected Mom's photo of European row houses tucked up against a cement pier. Mom chose a moody sky and water scene. Our friend, Norma, had a beach scene from a recent trip to Hawaii.

Creativity in a group is both calming and exciting. Unlike athletics, the energy hums between the participants. Each of us set up 'studio' space around the dining room table. Mom's ruler, needed for her new skills with perspective. Norma's paintbrushes like at Paint Nite. Caitlyn with her and a bunch of paint colors – for inspiration. I had a picture – supplies were yet to be determined.

"I wondered what Grandma was going to do with that ruler," said Caitlyn. "I thought of this as a casual session to create, and I wondered if she felt like we were giving her homework. It's the way she is, more precise than I could ever be. It worked, the painting looked just like the photo."

Using Caitlyn as my guide, I let go of my fear of failure. I went out of my comfort zone with a simplified graphic style, as you might see on the cover of New Yorker Magazine. It was freeing. For the next three days, I kept adding cut out paper figures to create a collage.

Mom worked the paint with wadded paper capturing the motion of the clouds. Norma's relaxed strokes created beautiful driftwood as she shared stories about her Hawaii trip. I kept looking a Caitlyn, with her feet on the table holding her camper at odd angles. I thought a lot about my aunt Ava, an award-winning artist, and how she also lets the paint fly.

Over coffee the next morning, we talked about the experience. Mom and Norma agreed that is was uncomfortable in the beginning, but they relaxed as the evening progressed. The tension early in the evening came from finding an approach to doing something new.

My row houses and funny people hang in my office. Each time I look at it, memories of that evening come flooding back. I see a better, more original version of myself because of everything we are doing together. We are nurturing each other's creativity and providing a space to grow as individuals.

Upcycling Challenge.

Caitlyn challenged us to upcycle a thrift store item. Her rules were simple: spend $10 on an item, $10 for embellishments, and use any craft items in the house. The transformed piece had to be displayed or posted on the 'Pinterest Fail' page.

This challenge makes each person equally engaged when shopping. It is distinctly different than helping someone shop for a dress, where the focus is on one person or wandering around the mall, where there is no focus. At the store, you may choose to act as comrades, conferring on pieces, and suggesting improvements. You may want to be competitors, hiding the best items. In either case, everyone is engaged.

Mom was home, recovering from a cross country skiing accident, so we texted her pictures of upcycling candidates. Caitlyn and I chose to be comrades and filled the cart with merchandise. It took longer to re-shelve all of our rejects than it did to select the objects.

At the craft store, we grabbed on sale paint and decorative items. In a funny twist, mom upcycled one of the embellishments rather than the project piece.

Artistic pursuits, like drawing, painting, or spatial planning, use the right side of the brain. Talking, writing, or recognizing an object by name, uses the left side of the brain. The room would get quiet, almost meditative, as we were using the right side of our minds. Then someone would ask a question, and we'd all start talking at once.

Caitlyn's project changed a couple of times throughout the evening. Mom's use of kitchen supplies for success was clever. When I chose a metal woven basket, I thought I would be creating something with a modern vibe, but it was Victorian. I was procrastinating, so Mom and Caitlyn jumped in with ideas. I chose to surrender to their imaginations and enjoyed the experience. It was liberating.

__Caitlyn:__ I didn't think Grandma would be into this challenge. I know she's not a fan of thrift stores and has everything she could ever need in her home. But she jumped in, picking a project and making it work. Unlike my mom, I like being creative with other people. She can spend hours in a small room sewing or writing, but I like having others around. We are talking and laughing together. It makes me feel close, and it gives me much needed adult time after spending the day with a two-year-old.

I like sharing stories, but I'm very tactile, so doing something hands-on is more fun for me. I also like that we are all taking risks and trying things. I believe I'm loosening Grandma up. On one challenge, she painted an eye in the sky, staring at snakes in the river.

These are times we will all remember. I have to confess that I feel like Mom and Grandma interact with each other more than with me, but I believe it's just because they are more naturally on the same wavelength and probably because they are older. I still like hanging with them.

Experts say when you exercise; the body continues to experience benefits for hours. We found that after these creative activities, our minds continued to experience the benefits of relaxation and rejuvenation. New neuro-connections opened the door to being creative in new ways. These gals have tamped down the judgmental side of my mind that often stops me from growing as an artist.

Overpainting a Thrift Store Find.

Caitlyn's next creative challenge for the Generation Gals was to give new life and a new look to a painting found at the thrift store. She discovered this idea on YouTube watching artist Kasey Golden transform oil paintings. The three of us watched Kasey paint ghosts on a fall landscape scene and aliens in a forest. She put her artistic stamp on someone else's work.

It took a few trips to find oil and acrylic paintings that fit our project budget – meaning cheap – but we found them. They sat behind the door in the art room for months as the summer weather drew us outside. Like all friends, we make plans and take months to follow through.

Canvases were randomly assigned a week before our painting night. I always think of my Aunt Ava and how she gives you the confidence to set aside your fear of failure and let your imagination run.

I felt guilty about painting on someone else's work until my paintbrush made the first stroke. Mom and Caitlyn never felt that concern. Mom kept saying that she was taking a painting no one wanted and turning it into a picture no one would want to hang – guilt-free.

I was most surprised by Mom's creativity. The canvas was a forest landscape with a river running through it. She painted a giant eye in the sky, sending streaks of light into the woodlands below. A woman sat on a rock basking in the eye's glory while snakes danced in the frothing waters.

"All the work I've been doing with my photography, studying light, and looking at lots of pictures, combined with our projects, has made me more willing just to have fun with paints," said Lois.

I must admit that I feel awed and a little competitive. Mom's imagination has grown faster than mine. I am working my creative muscles harder, so I can keep up.

"I want a landscape next time because you can make more happen," said Caitlyn. "My favorite part was having people tell me what to add to the picture while I was working on it."

Caitlyn's picture was two wine bottles and a glass of wine. She glued a drinking straw to look as if it was coming out of the wine glass with a stick figure poised to drink. She had small people climbing the bottles and parachuting off. At the bottom, she drew drunks spray-painting graffiti and others playing the piano.

I had a fall landscape that made me think of Halloween. I painted witches coming in for a celebration focusing on a raging fire.

We had fun with it, stretched our creative muscles, and spent some time as friends. It was so relaxed and different than anything we had ever done before. Mom found a corner in the bathroom to hang all three works. You can't ask for more than that!

TWELVE
COMMUNITY EVENTS

For us, community events are either famine or feast. In Alaska, the depths of winter are dark and cold, so December through February is a time of social hibernation. We only have about five hours of sunlight a day. Come March; we are all bursting to get out. The days are twelve to fifteen hours, and the temperatures are climbing into the '30s. Sunlight changes 7 minutes per day as we head toward July and almost 24 hours of daylight.

We all, mother-daughter-granddaughter, pour over the event listings choosing old standards and something new. It's easy to get into a rut because it takes a little more planning to attend a new event. Our goal is to mix old and new.

We can be spur-of-the-moment people, but this challenge is better with a little planning. I felt like I was letting Caitlyn down because, at 23, she's ready to go anytime. Planning a few weeks out, and making busy weeks off-limits reduced my guilt. We did more because we were looking at the schedule of events.

An Old Favorite.

Every region has a few favorite local events. The annual World Ice Art Championships is Fairbanks' gem event. Artists from Asia, Russia, Europe, and America transform blocks of ice into gravity-defying sculptures, intricate mazes, animals, and toys for a children's play park complete with slides. Sculptures from 5 feet by 5 feet to those fifteen feet tall by twenty feet long are on display. The artists come to Fairbanks because we have the best ice in the world.

During the day, the park is a playland with children weaving in and out of ice mazes, spinning in ice teacups, crawling through ice trains, and sliding on a dozen slides. Houses, complete with ice benches and ice beds, stand beside ice bears bringing to mind children's stories.

At night the park's atmosphere transforms, colorfully lit sculptures sitting along forest paths take on an ethereal quality. It's like walking in a painting - the sky, trees, ice, and lighting combine to carry you away. Artists can sculpt anything, so visitors move from abstract images to perfect replicas of sea creatures. There are fifteen-foot horses with manes flying, two-story terracotta soldiers standing poised for battle, and snow machines racing through a forest scene.

Fairbanks comes together for the festival. Go into any coffee shop, and you will hear debates about the most beautiful or the strangest sculpture. It brings us together – creating a shared memory – for Alaskans. These events are about 'being there' and are talked about for years.

If you have not attended your community's highlight event for a few years, grab someone, and go. I believe you will feel closer to your neighbors after sharing the experience.

Finding a New Community Experience.
When people come to visit, we pull out brochures and calendars to fill their visit with exciting activities. We decided to treat ourselves as travelers and do something new.

We attended the Nenana Ice Classic. Nenana is an hour and a half from Fairbanks. At the edge of town is a trestle bridge that crosses the Tanana River. In 1917, railroad engineers began to bet on when the Tanana river ice would melt enough to see the water flowing. Locals built a tripod in the center of the river. They strung a thin cable to a timer onshore. When the tripod shifted, the timer stopped - capturing the exact moment. The engineer who guessed correctly - won the pot of money.

This tradition continues today, and anyone can enter for $2.50 per guess. More than $4 million worth of tickets have been purchased. Last year, the pot was $225,000, and the winners each received almost $6,500. We buy tickets and watch for the date of breakup, but none of us had attended the annual festival to set the tripod.

Mom, Caitlyn, Cordell and I loaded ourselves into the car and headed over the mountain pass to Nenana. The event is a spring celebration with activities indoors and outdoors. We'd shed our coats and snow pants in the community center to watch magic shows, demonstrations of traditional native sports, shop for local crafts, and eat. Then we'd bundle up to head outside for a tug-o-war with locals vs. visitors (the visitors lost) and general snow play.

Everyone goes onto the river to help set up the thirty-foot tall tripod. Visitors can assist or watch from the ice block seats. I helped while Mom photographed, and Cordell climbed beyond the wall of blocks and ran down the river. We stopped to stare as a musher, with a full team, went gliding past.

 When the tripod went up, I was sharing a moment with those early railroad men. I felt connected with those early settlers amusing themselves over the long winter. Are we any different now? Don't we find ways to make life enjoyable, to have things to talk about, and to create activities to share?

The event closed with something we had never seen - a Pop Drop for the kids. They spread cases of individual soda cans in the street, and the kids ran down with their shopping bags to gather their favorite flavors. (I heard from an old-timer that it started decades ago with cases of beer.) Kids were hunting for orange and trading for a root beer. Cordell left with a bag full of fizzy sugary fun!

Facebook Events is a great place to find new activities happening in your area.

Celebrate the End of the Adventure.
We closed the Nenana Ice Classic day at Monderosa's for Caitlyn's favorite hamburgers. Could we have gone home and called it a successful day? Of course, but closing rituals are that cherry on top - making the day that much more special.

I have traveled down new roads. I have visited quaint farms, stunning greenhouses, fields of flowers, and historic neighborhoods I never knew existed because we committed to connecting with the community.

THIRTEEN
CONNECTING TO THE FAMILY TREE

I keep mentioning my fascination with time. I spend time trying to hold on to the present, connect with the past, and anticipate the future. Songwriters, Josh Kear, David Frasier, and Ed Hill were speaking right to me with the sentence, "I believe that days go so slow and years go fast." Living in the moment extends the experience, but when I look forward or back, life flies past at a speed that makes my head spin.

According to Stacey Colino, author of 'How Nostalgia Can Be Good for Your Health and Well-Being' [10], nostalgic recollection connects our past to our present self. In weaving the threads of our lives together, we restore a sense of personal identity. It can help you with problem-solving, give greater meaning to your life, and improve your relationships.

Looking back can bring the past into the present for a little while. Reminiscing, listening to music from your youth, looking at old photos are all good for you, and sharing memories about a time or a place with someone who had similar experiences helps us live longer, healthier lives. Sharing our experiences, along with our feelings at the time, gives our children and adult grandchildren a view of us as a whole person. Memories connect us, inform us, and provide us with context for who we are today.

Share moments that shaped your attitudes.
At a reunion, my cousin and I were talking about the women we loved

and respected. I brought up one of my favorite memories of her mother.

When we were six or seven, my aunt would sit down in the rocking chair and turn on a single small lamp at her shoulder. A few millers would fly toward the light, attracted to my aunt just like us six kids. She was a hard-working woman with a farm and nine children, but in those moments, she was a star. She would take out her dentures and start talking in a character's voice. We laughed for hours – well, maybe it was only thirty minutes. I loved how she would set aside a woman's typical vanity to entertain a half-dozen children.

My cousin's reaction to our shared memory – so enthusiastic and knowing – instantly took both of us to that small patch of light in a darkened living room. Our shared energy generated the visceral feeling.

Personal memories are things that happened to make us who we are today. They are the memories we draw on to relate to others, to empathize, to get frustrated, or to understand. We filter our experiences through our personal beliefs and our faith. We are our memories. Sharing these helps us go from the stereotypic role of mother or grandmother or daughter to adults who are friends. It also helps us feel less alone.

"Yes, I have cried at work before…it makes you tougher," said my mother, one day early in my career. This statement from a woman who never cries, sharing her memory of being vulnerable, gave me strength and confidence while making her more human.

"I hate the first time I go to any event. I watch and do not talk to anyone," I explain to Caitlyn, who hates crowds. "I am gregarious and outgoing, but only after I get to know you – so large gatherings are very stressful until I attend two or three times."

"I was not a good housekeeper when I was young," Mom says. "It was Cathy's dad that got me into a routine of cleaning on Saturday and keeping one room ready for company." Mom brought this up when I was grumbling to Caitlyn about the state of the house.

Incidents that shaped us overtime are powerful once our children become adults. You don't need to share every moment or every doubt. The goal is sharing empathetically, to let your adult child know they are not alone, or to let them into your life as an equal adult. These are not parables, teaching us a moral lesson; these are stories about living an adult life in the best way we can.

Picture opening the curtains and letting us peek in the windows. My sister,

Linda, has a gift for this type of sharing. She begins by humanizing herself or the person featured in the memory: "I know she had to be …." or "He must have been feeling so …" and then she shares what happened. "I didn't appreciate living in the country when I was in my twenties, and I wanted to be in town. It wasn't a long drive, but it seemed like it was at the time."

Caitlyn and I disagree about the best way to share reminiscences. I love when little recollections are dropped in conversation – 'that reminds me of a time when.' Caitlyn feels memories shared in this way can get lost in the conversation and will not stay with us. I agree that we do not remember these stories as well, but I enjoy the texture they add to our general lives. Caitlyn enjoys setting up situations that allow us to focus on those stories.

We started by sharing memories around the table on random evenings or driving in the car. Now, these personal memories flow freely between the three of us. Caitlyn, Mom, and I share equally. Caitlyn uses examples of things that happened recently to identify with Mom's frustration with her new phone. Mom tells stories about being a single mother of two boys. Mom and I discuss my work, which is similar to her career, with tales of triumph and frustration.

We put on music from various eras and dance. What I enjoy most is that we listen. Peeking into the stories that shaped us does not stop us from getting frustrated or mad, but the anger is not as intense, and the time to bounce back to friendship is much shorter.

Reminiscing Is Healthy.
Historically, reminiscing was tied to depression. Thought leaders believed that anyone looking back at happy moments must not be satisfied now. I wonder how the listener's insecurities fed into this myth. When my daughter talks about her love Iowa or shares memories of picking apples with her nieces in New Hampshire, I become insecure. I feel that she is choosing her past life over her current life. I wonder if I have made a series of mistakes. I have to remind myself that she is sharing – not comparing.

In The *New York Times* article, 'What is Nostalgia Good For? Quite a Bit, Research Shows'[11], author John Tierney introduces us to enthusiastic nostalgia researchers: Dr. Constantine Sedikides and Dr. Erica Hepper. Dr. Sedikides became interested in the subject when a friend suggested that his desire to talk about past homes and experiences might be a sign of depression. Dr. Sedikides enjoyed reminiscing and knew he was not depressed, so his friend's reaction led him to study nostalgia in-depth for decades. He points out that not all memories are happy ones, but the positive elements greatly outweigh the negative.

Dr. Hepper shares that nostalgia levels tend to be high among young adults, then dip in middle age and rise again during old age. "Nostalgia helps us deal with transitions," she says. Examples include students leaving home after high school, parents becoming empty nesters, and individuals retiring.

"Nostalgia makes us a bit more human." Dr. Sedikides said. He created a nostalgic repository of memories to lift his spirits and give him confidence. "I don't miss an opportunity to build nostalgic-to-be memories. We call this anticipatory nostalgia," Dr. Sedikides said.

Lois: I've been more nostalgic about my youth since we started this process. The funny thing is, there are segments of time where I don't remember interacting with all members of my family. My parents' first three children — my sister, brother, and I — were born within three years. It was seven years before my two brothers came along. My youngest sister and my son are the same age, so she is seventeen years younger than me. I remember my youngest brothers until I reach high school, and then my focus must have shifted. They become the two boys playing together, off-screen from my life's main events.

The Comparative Memory Game.

What does it mean that our memory is selective? Does it say we love particular people less? Why are some shared memories in perfect synch while only one of us remembers others? Catherine de Lange's article, 'How can two people recall an event so differently?'[12], NewScientist.com shines a light on selective memory. Dr. Signy Sheldon at McGill University studied how our brains store and retrieve memories. Those who are better at remembering facts had more links in areas of the brain involved in reasoning. Those with detailed autobiographical memories are more connected in the areas of visual processing. Emotional connections to the memory count. Sheldon says, "Emotional events can be recalled much more naturally, almost like they are stamped in our minds."

Caitlyn: I remember in full color. The emotions are electric and feel like they are happening now. Mom and I have some memories where we can finish the other's description of the action. On a trip to Boston, my older brother, Gregor, was wearing a kilt. Frustrated at trying to get a decent picture, Mom said, "I either want to see your smiling face or your backside." My brother flipped up his kilt and mooned her in one of the funniest moments ever. We both remember this moment with perfect clarity. But, when I mention learning to make maple syrup together, she draws a complete blank. She was one of the Girl Scout leaders, and I know she was there, but we couldn't count on her to tap a tree.

In an experiment, Mom and I began comparing memories. I reminded her of our coldest weekend skiing ever. I described my horror when a fellow skier's toenails turned black after a shower. Mom remembers that it was so cold her ski tip broke off on the top of a mogul. She climbed back up to the ski lift and rode down in a chair. I don't remember her having to rent gear for the weekend, but we both remember the cold.

This comparative memory game is entertaining. It passes the time when driving, walking, or cleaning the kitchen. The experiences can be funny or touching. These memories reinforce our similarities and differences.

Memories are also powerful for those who did not share the experience. In the magazine, *How To Be An Awesome Grandparent*, September 2019[16], Daria Price Bowman shares, "Kids grow up happier when they have a sense of their roots. Now is the time to bring your family history to life!" Connections to the past help us understand who we are now.

My Great Uncle Malinski was an influential farmer in southeastern Colorado from the 1930s–1980s. He wrote or consulted on many of the water laws and opinions about water laws that shaped eastern plains agriculture. In his small town, there was one paved road off the highway, and the pavement ended at his driveway. My son, Gregor, is an environmental lawyer and volunteers many hours to water law causes. He studied his great-great uncle's papers and books and shares that relationship with pride. He connects with a man he never met and wants to build on our family legacy.

The Power of a Story.

The television show *Finding Your Roots* sets people on a path to find the legendary stories of their ancestors. We look for more than names and faces; we look for the stories that transcend time – connecting us to our parents, grandparents, and beyond.

I love family legends. These stories draw on a robust oral history used to pass them from generation to generation. In large families, hundreds of cousins, second cousins, and distant relations know these tales. Legends are often repeated and probably embellished by the story-teller, but they hold a kernel of truth at their center.

My favorite family legend is about how my grandparents met – first connections are always so special. My grandfather moved from Texas to the

Colorado plains in the late 1920s. His nephew came home with news about the pretty school teacher, just off the train from Missouri. The next day, my grandfather rode his horse into the one-room schoolhouse to get a glimpse of this young lady. Grandma grabbed the broom and with her best schoolmarm diction, shooed that man and his horse out the door. This story has all of the makings of a legend – old-west location, boy meets girl, tension, a horse, and a broom.

"This explains so much about Grandma Lois. Now I understand why she doesn't take crap from anyone. She inherited that trait from my great-grandma," Caitlyn said after a storytelling session.

Family legends often depict heroism, bravery, generosity, or humor. The hero or heroine experience something larger than life. In the Disney movie "Moana," a tribal legend affirms a teenager's love of the water and gives her the strength to begin a quest to save her people. For Ragu Spaghetti sauce, the family legend is about Mrs. Cantisano selling jars of sauce from her front porch in 1937.

Another of our legends is about my mother. As a teenager, she competed in a weeklong rodeo near the family homestead on the southeastern plains of Colorado. The family was financially strapped; Mom would say – poor. She didn't own fancy big horses like the girl competitors, so she knew she couldn't win competing in the girls' events. Since the competitor with the most points wins and boys' events were worth more points than girls' events - Mom competed against the boys. To win the overall cowgirl award, she would need to do well in the last contest, a three-horse relay. It was impossible to win without three fast horses, so a local rancher and friend of my grandfather's offered to lend some horses.

The three quarter-horses were lined up along the course for the final relay event. Competitors would race a quarter-mile, complete a jumping dismount on the dusty track, and then a running mount holding the saddle horn of the next horse. As Mom was mounting the last horse, her bra broke, but she didn't stop. She won the relay with that bra-snapping in the wind behind her and was named the overall cowgirl. A newspaper artist drew her leaning forward in the saddle, waving the flag of womanhood. How could any of us give up after hearing this tale of grit, determination, and victory?

Some stories live forever, while others disappear after a few generations. Family members telling the story, again and again, make these endure. I try to share our family legends because it is the golden rope that winds through my vast family tree. Our family historians have inspiring stories I have not read, so I know I can to add more legends to my repertoire.

Bringing Stories to Life.

The great stories in my family are short and easy to remember. The best part is you don't have to be a great writer – in fact – these are oral histories, so you don't have to write at all. You only need to be able to tell a story and show a picture. A few simple rules bring stories to life.

Know Your Audience.

Throughout my childhood, my mother and aunts would pull out the big box of photos at my grandparent's house and pass them around the waxed kitchen tablecloth like cards in a game of rummy. They would turn the black and white images so everyone could see and talk about the participants, which would lead to more stories and a lot of laughing. The blue ballpoint pen would come out if the names were missing from the back. I do not remember my great Aunt Maime, but I can pick her out in a photograph.

I remember these nights fondly; however, my attention would wander because I could not connect with many of these memories. I noticed the same teenage behavior at our family reunions. These kids are busy making memories, and when the conversation moves to relatives they never met, they drift away. They didn't feel the energy from that shared connection. It is the equivalent of going to a neighbor's house to look at family photos.

Young people need more information to connect to the people in the photograph. You need to draw in your audience.

Create a Picture of the Main Character.

Use comparisons, maybe the person in the photo looks like an audience member. If you do not have family pictures, or you do not know what the person looks like, then use the preface, "I assume or I bet." Here are some examples:

Your great-grandfather Sam had your dimples when he smiled and used them to his advantage.

Your great-aunt Millie was only four-foot ten inches, but her hairdo made her look six feet tall.

Your grandpa Rick was a dare-devil. Every time I see you play, I think of him.

I have never seen a picture of great-great-great grandpa Joseph, but I assume he had dark hair, just like your momma. From the stories I've heard, I'm guessing he had a lot of laugh lines around his eyes, just like me.

Think about the Historical Setting.

Is the story in the early 1900s or the 1970s? Is there something happening at that point in history that is important to the story or relevant to you? Going from New York to California does not seem difficult now, but in 1910 it would have been. Here are some examples:

At the end of World War II, we didn't have much because the government rationed food and paper products. Your great grandmother, Dawn, was shocked when kids in town started throwing rolls of toilet paper to celebrate victory in Europe on V-E Day.

Great-grandpa Karl came from Texas to Kansas in 1915. Just imagine, no cars, no highways, and drive-thru restaurants. He and his brothers had a team of horses pulling a wagon-like you see in the movies. Only one man could ride on the wagon at a time, so the other four had to walk. At night, they would stop to pitch a tent and build a fire. No one traveled at night.

The example of traveling from Texas to Kansas is a good one for telling the story of your family migration. You may not know the details, but you can share what travel was like at that time. I know my grandmother and her sisters traveled to Colorado by train. I can do a little research on what women moving alone in the late 1920s encountered and bring that snippet of information to life.

Share What They Were Feeling.

Do this directly or indirectly. I could have been more direct about mom's feelings in the story about the rodeo. She wanted to win, not only for the prize but to prove her worth. If you are telling stories to children, you have to be more direct, so I would say, "Grandma wanted to win that prize and show she was a great horsewoman, even if she didn't own a fancy horse." Here is an example for adults/teens and children:

Grandma Kelly had tears in her eyes when grandpa Joe left for the war. Grandma

Kelly never cried; she always said tears were a waste of good water.

For kids: Grandma Kelly was so sad and afraid when grandpa Joe left for the war. She was worried about grandpa Joe, and she knew she would be so lonely waiting for him to come home. She never cried, but there were tears in her eyes that day.

Use Action or Humor or Both.

There are no family legends about the couch potato uncle watching television incessantly – unless something funny happened to the remote. Action is more about moving and less about details. Make your listeners feel like they are there.

Aunt Evelyn was screaming and waving her arms as the bear rushed grandpa Earl. She had seen him unsuccessfully trying to get a shell into the rifle. [Start waiving your arms and mimicking loading a gun at this point.] Could she distract it long enough for grandpa to load the rifle and shoot? The bear looked big on the trail, but now headed in their direction, it seems enormous. Evelyn is worried that if she starts to run, grandpa will think she's abandoning him, not drawing the bear away. Grandpa Earl is yanking on his rifle, and it's jammed. It's not a rifle anymore. The bear is so close, Evelyn has to look up to see its face. [At this point, look up toward the top of the windows with your arms in the air.] Grandpa Earl is now swinging the rifle in the air, yelling, "What should we do?"

If there are children in the audience, have them wave their arms in the air and ask them, "What should Grandpa and Aunt Evelyn do?" Then finish the story with a flourish.

Sedate stories depend on humor, emotion, or poignancy. Stories of helping others are an excellent place for fun. Maybe there was irony, for example, someone unable to read trying to help a blind person order off a menu. Another example of irony is when one individual from the city tells his companion the perfect spot to set up a tent in the woods.

Use the Five Senses.

Everyone connects differently to a story, so remember the five senses: sight, hearing, touch, taste, and smell. See if you can include a couple of senses in your story. This example is my favorite paragraph from my Uncle Johnnie Allen's story 'The Good Old Days' from his book, *Uneventful Events.*[13] Set in late November 1938, the three children have just listened to a scary story on the radio.

It was bedtime, after a quick trip outside for comfort relief, then off to the cold room, and the bed piled high with comforters. A rapid jump into pajamas and nightgowns, then three in a bed, shivering, trying to warm up the blanket as they huddled together. Mom comes into the cold bedroom and issues goodnight kisses, then as the coyotes howl and the wind moans, they try to erase the grisly story they've just heard.

Johnnie was able to draw on three senses in one paragraph. It was cold - touch. Coyotes howling and wind moaning - hearing. They huddled together - sight. There's humor in the description of going to the bathroom, and there is poignancy in the goodnight kiss – which was probably fast because their mother was cold.

Interview Family.

Sit and talk with your parents or aunts/uncles or read the family history to find legends and stories. These stories may not be fully formed, so ask questions to learn more.

First Meeting or Date Questions.

Were you nervous? What part of the person did your notice first (hair, eyes, clothes)? Was it cold or hot or raining? Did you use a mint or mouth spray just before the meeting? What was your first impression?

Adventure Questions.

What scared you most? Were you palms sweating, or were you nauseous? What were you thinking then, and what do you feel now? Was the weather hot or cold? Did you win or lose? How did those around you react – were they laughing, helping, running away?

What About World Events?

Was there something political or economic that drove you to make a change? How did it feel to be arrested for protesting? What did the handcuffs feel like on your wrists? How would you feel about young people today protesting?

Story Gathering Gets Easier with Practice.

The more you know about your family and the era, the easier it is to gather the story and share it. Check out the National Storytelling Network, storynet.org, if you would like to learn more.

FOURTEEN
OTHER WAYS TO SHARE THE PAST

Our personal stories may not live up to family legend status, but we still need to share them and hear them. There are a lot of journals available with questions designed to help you record your life to share later with your grandchildren. Some journals have space for the grandparent and the grandchild to work together. I am guessing that many of these remain untouched - it's not that we do not care - it is that writing a life story is a daunting task, and daily journaling can seem boring or trivial.

How do we determine what to share? If you think about a book store, there are hundreds of choices of stories. Everyone in the store is not lined up in a single section. Some people love mysteries, others cookbooks, others non-fiction, others political, other religious – you get the idea. The best stories connect with the listener. Helping each other tell engaging stories binds us together.

Ask about Times and Activities that Interest You.

Inquire about the times and events that interest your listeners. A topic may be too big to get a good story. What was it like during World War II? Narrow the question based on your interests. Did you have a victory garden during World War II? What was it like to use ration books?

Question and answer can be a hit or miss game. The person answering can help by giving ideas if they do not have a relevant memory.

Me: "Did you have a victory garden during World War II?"

Mom: "No, they were in the cities. We always just had a garden. Would you like to know about our garden or can I tell you about Rosie the Riveter? Her reputation was a little risqué."

Me: "Absolutely. You know I want any story about the beginnings of women in the workforce." I could have replied that I wanted to hear about the garden and asked if she grew the same things they did in a victory garden?

Sell Your Story.

If you want to share something, use a little salesmanship and include the parts of the tale that will interest your audience. Be careful here - remember this is a story between friends. These are not moral tales about the value of work or how geography was different when you were young because you had to walk uphill both ways to school.

Once Upon an Eskimo Time by Edna Wilder[16] is a gift of sharing by both a mother and daughter. Wilder wanted to write about her mother's early life in Alaska, around 1868, before white people came to her village. Wilder's mother, at more than 110 years old, told tales of her childhood. Wilder wanted her sons to know what it was like to live without electricity, cars, or stores. She was interested in the tales her mother had to tell.

Mom would like to capture how her brothers and sisters viewed each other as children. We will have each brother or sister tell stories about another sibling. I'll collect these and then decide what to do with them. I am hoping this collection of stories is the perfect Valentine's gift for my mother. It is a mystery project that sounds like fun!

The Children's Book Project.

If your grandchild or great-grandchild is younger, consider working together on a children's book – just for the family. Choose a topic that interests the child. If she loves the ocean, make the book about your swim with dolphins. If he loves to sew, make a quilt book. A kid who owns hot wheels will want to hear about your convertible with four-on-the-floor. Write a four-page story with one, two, or three sentences per page and add photos.

Create the Unbook.

We don't need to write a book. Write Post-It notes of things that were different in the past or surprising things that are the same. Stick them in a journal with some tape and voila - it's a book. Record an audio or video with your phone. Make the clips short because there is a variety of easy-to-use software to splice them together later. Seem too difficult? The box of photos on the kitchen table has served us well.

Sharing Through Food.

Smell is the most robust sense associated with memory, which is why certain meals "take you back to grandma's house" or why the scent of rain transports me to a former home in New Hampshire. Sometimes my husband uses the percolator, and when it begins to bubble, I daydream of waking in a tent by the lake.

"Recipes are the best way to share memories!" Caitlyn said. "I feel most connected when I'm doing something with Grandma, and recipes let me feel that again and again." My daughter cares less about the exact recipe and more about the movements we make in the kitchen. "It doesn't matter what type of cake I'm making, helping with Grandma's four-layer German Chocolate cake comes to mind." Like art, cooking gives the mind room to wander down pathways in our memories.

My best friend's son, now in his thirties, still talks about the filet steak hot dogs my husband made him when he was young. When I drink cordials, I remember a friend's Christmas Kahlua. Hopefully, as my granddaughters get older, they will remember my husband, Brent, feeding them chocolate chips – a scoop for the dough and a few for you.

Brent fulfilled our granddaughter's wish when he made Rabbit Stew one Christmas eve. The next year he Federal Expressed a frozen rabbit and the recipe.

Share Stories When You are Cooking and Cook to Tell Stories.

We all agree that food makes connections. Cooking can inspire conversations on a wide variety of topics. Look beyond the recipe to ingredients, places, events, or daily activities. What foods were abundant when you were growing up? What were you forced to eat that you didn't like?

How were you feeling at particular moments in time, and how did that shape who you are now? When I was divorcing my first husband, my son and I ate macaroni and cheese – from the blue box – with hotdogs and peas, night after night. My career was going well, but I was young, and money was tight. I could have felt like a failure for these cheap meals, but I didn't. I felt in control of my finances and how I spent every dime. I haven't always felt that way through the years, but today I still feel powerful knowing I could go back to two-dollar meals if needed.

Go on a journey with a meal. Cook something memorable and describe the adventure or get take out if you can't recreate the meal. Share photos while you eat. When my husband cooks seafood, he describes in graphic detail the giant Maine lobsters crawling across our New Hampshire kitchen floor.

Create a Recipe Book with Photos of the Cooks.

The recipe doesn't have to be a family recipe. If Uncle Joe made meatloaf from a Betty Crocker Cookbook, copy the recipe onto a card or a page and include a photo of Joe. If there is room, write a few lines with a food-related memory of the relative. Here's an example:

'Grandpa Chip would always eat eggs scrambled with cheese before fishing' is the perfect statement for a Cheese and Spinach Scramble. Glue Grandpa's picture to the card or draw a little fishing pole, and you've preserved a memory.

A box of recipes can also be unique. When I moved out on my own for the first time, my sister gave me a recipe box with a collection of recipes that were easy to make and easy on the budget. I often think of that collection of handwritten cards – like love notes from home. If the recipe is from a magazine, cut it out and glue it. This activity should be fun and easy.

In the spirit of creating nostalgic moments, make the recipes together, and talk about the family members who ate around the table all those years ago. Caitlyn reminds us again to bring out the pictures. We didn't have the full kitchen with everyone cooking very often – if you do – I tip my hat to you!

Share Your Talents and Crafts.

"Sewing!" is Caitlyn's second suggestion. You can see why she features prominently in the creative section of the book.

__Caitlyn:__ I learned so much about grandma and the past on the day she sewed for me. I was in middle school and wanted a straight skirt. She laid the newspaper on the table, grabbed a marker, and started drawing. I have never seen anyone freehand a pattern except on Project Runway. Years later, my Aunt Linda told me about a time when Grandma made a four-piece outfit for a trip while she was going to college, working, and taking care *of a small child. I see where mom gets her love of fabric, and I get my love of clothes. To this day, I can't believe how grandma whipped out that skirt.*

There are mother-daughter teams who work on fabric art together. The daughter begins with a fabric canvas. The mother takes the canvas and adds embellishments. We have not tried this yet, but I'm excited to see what collaboration could bring.

The list of crafting activities is long: gardening, making jam, canning, playing piano, building models, or working on cars. Too often, we assume the other person is not interested, when it may be that the timing is a problem, so ask. If you are asked to do something new, say yes because you are curious, not because you feel you must help.

Sharing Places.
Visit places from your past or your family's past together. Traveling as adult friends can be challenging and rewarding. It works when you set expectations and try to live up to them. My life is very hectic, so travel must include some downtime. Mom has more energy than all of us, so she is always ready to explore. We set aside time to explore and time to rest. Mom and I also go for a long walk every morning or evening - don't forget to stay in shape. Caitlyn has a young child, so we need to accommodate toddler time. Each person enjoys different experiences - hiking, museums, sleeping-in, meeting new people, or going dancing.

Visiting places from the past also needs to include new experiences shared between you and your companions to create new nostalgic opportunities. Travel is a time to be open to new experiences.

Base Games on Your Family.
Create a Trivial Pursuit game that stars your family. Each generation can add cards. One side of the card has a question about a family member, and the other side has a list of possible answers.

The game Two Truths and a Lie is another fun way to share memories. You tell three stories. Two of the stories are true, and one is a lie. The other players have to guess which story is the lie.

My friend Deby plays Rummy. They name certain combinations of cards after family members. "If you have kept a hand with a low point count, we call that an Aunt Lilly," Deby said. "She always held the lowest hands when she played. We have family names for many of the hands. It lets us remember people near and dear."

Play Risk and change the rules for countries you have visited or those that have ancestral connections. Try Risk with a US map and tie in family history.

Photographs Work.

Let's go to the pictures – literally. I love the box of images, even in this digital age. I still have photo albums and scrapbooks full of pictures from when my children were young. To me, sharing photos around the table is one of the most fun ways to connect our generations.

We plan to print pictures and collage so Caitlyn can learn about her family while creating an updated album. A collage is an art piece that has photographs, fabric, writing, and/or drawings glued to paper, canvas, or fabric. There is no photo of my grandfather in the schoolhouse on a horse, but a collage with the building (or one like it), a photo of my grandfather riding and my grandmother as a girl will capture the story. A picture of a broom from a magazine, a piece of fabric from that era and a photo of grandma and grandpa together will complete the work of art.

Celebrate Your Family Member's and Ancestors' Differences.

Friends accept each other. Celebrate your differences when sharing memories. Our memories are vulnerable to change each time we revisit an event or a person. Memory is like the telephone game, with each retelling, story parts that are misheard or misunderstood, and alter the original memory. I hope you can avoid doing that with stories that can showcase the diversity of culture, ideas, religion, race, ethnicity, or sexual orientation in your family tree. Going back to the bookstore analogy, that relative who was different may be the one person connecting a loved one to your family tree.

LIST OF SOURCES

[1] **Hadden, Jeff**, "This Study of 300,000 People Reveals the 1 Secret to Living a Longer, Healthier Life," Inc.com, 17 October 2017, https://www.inc.com/jeff-haden/this-study-of-300000-people-reveals-1-secret-to-living-a-longer-healthier-life.html

[2] **Schaefer Riley**, Naomi, "Want to live longer? Choose family over friends." NYPost.com, 27 August 2016, https://nypost.com/2016/08/27/want-to-live-longer-choose-family-over-friends/

[3] **Conville, Nicola**, "Friendships Make You Live Longer', bodyandsoul.com.au, 17 June 2016, News Pty., https://www.bodyandsoul.com.au/sex-relationships /relationships/friendships-make-you-live-longer/news-story/92e5dd3c24e71b86ca806ce2d17df1e4

[4] **Champan, Gary and Presson**, Ramon, 101 Conversation Starters for Families, 1 April 2012, Northfield Publishing

[5] **Cohut Ph.D., Maria**, 'What are the health benefits of being social?', Medical News Today, 23 February 2018, Health Media UK Ltd., https://www.medicalnewstoday.com/articles/320947.php

[6] **Bruni, Frank**. Interview with Betty White. Times Talk, New York Times – YouTube, 18 October 2012, https://www.youtube.com/watch?v=3LNjmo4Cbaw

[7] **Brice, Carleen**, 'The Benefits of Creativity for Older Adults.' DenverArtMuseum.org, 7 April 2015,
https://denverartmuseum.org/article/benefits-creativity-older-adults

[8] **Bagan Ph.D., Barbara**, 'Aging: What's Art Got To Do With It? TodaysGeriatricMedicine.com, Great Valley Publishing Company
https://www.todaysgeriatricmedicine.com/news/ex_082809_03.shtml

[9] **Siegel, Robert, Hsu, Andrea**, "Like Brain Boot Camp: Using Music to Ease Hearing Loss," All Things Considered, 31 May 2017, National Public Radio.
https://www.npr.org/sections/health-shots/2017/05/31/530723021/like-brain-boot-camp-using-music-to-ease-hearing-loss

[10] **Colino, Stacey**, 'How Nostalgia Can Be Good for Your Health and Well-Being', USNews.com, 26 December 18
https://health.usnews.com/wellness/mind/articles/2018-12-26/how-nostalgia-can-be-good-for-your-health-and-well-being

[11] **Tierney, John**, 'What is Nostalgia Good For? Quite a Bit, Research Shows' nytimes.com 8 July 2013, The New York Times,
https://www.nytimes.com/2013/07/09/science/what-is-nostalgia-good-for-quite-a-bit-research-shows.html

[12] **de Lange's, Catherine**, "How can two people recall an event so differently?" NewScientist.com, 24 October 2018,
https://www.newscientist.com/article/mg24032011-300-memory-special-how-can-two-people-recall-an-event-so-differently/

[13] **Allen, Johnnie**, Uneventful Events, 2014, Self-Published

ABOUT THE GENERATION GALS

Lois Buscher (mom)

Lois is a woman of action. At sixteen, she dropped out of high school to marry and went on to earn her GED, bachelor's degree, CPA, and master's degree. She was a competitive rodeo rider, scaled mountains, including Mexico's tallest, Pico de Orizaba, rock climbed in the Rockies and is an expert skier. In the 1980s, Lois headed to Alaska in her VW van. She found adventure dog mushing, climbing glaciers, commercial fishing, and as a volunteer paramedic supporting Flight for Life in a small village. She travels the world by planes, trains, and automobiles carrying her camera every step of the way.

Cathy Ewing (author)

Cathy is an outdoorswoman who also loves the process of creating art. She travelled the world talking about beer, won awards for her work in the early days of the Internet and built non-profit communities. As a professional agent of change, she works with teams in high-stress situations when interactions can be at their best and worst. These experiences make her aware of how family members unwittingly or knowingly steal each other's power and confidence. She tries daily to improve her relationships – knowing we are all just human.

Caitlyn Ewing (daughter)

Caitlyn is a young single mother, finding her way in the world. Animals are her passion, and she is studying to become a vet tech. She has to do something creative every day in the kitchen, with fabric or with her thrift store finds.

A Place for Notes, Ideas, and Activities

Statements That Push My Buttons and The Change Request
Example Statement: I could do that for you.
Change Request: I appreciate your help. If I am doing a chore, could you please ask, "What else can I do for you?" because I already have this chore handled.
Statement:
Statement:
Statement:
Statement:

A Place for Notes, Ideas and Activities

Getting Active in Ways You Like and A Plan to Make it Happen
Example Activity: Hiking
Making it Happen: Enter the Winter Hiking Challenge through the Parks and Recreation Department
Activity:
Activity:
Activity:
Activity:

A Place for Notes, Ideas and Activities

Events I Would Like to Attend and **The Dates We Need to Reserve**
Example Event: World Ice Art Championships
Dates: February 15 – March 31
Event:
Event:
Event:
Event:

A Place for Notes, Ideas and Activities

My Biggest Fears for You and Agreements to Relieve those Fears
Example Fear: You will forget to take your medicine.
Honesty Agreement: I will use daily pill keepers, so I will know if I forget, and you will feel more comfortable about this.
Fear:
Fear:
Fear:
Fear:

A Place for Notes, Ideas and Activities

Ways to be Creative and Supplies to Pick Up or Order
Example Creative Activity: Family Collage
Supplies: Canvas or Hardboard, Photos of Grandparents and Great Aunts and Uncles, Markers, Sealant, Collage Magazine for Ideas
Activity:
Activity:
Activity:
Activity:

A Place for Notes, Ideas and Activities

Who is in The Family Tree and What Stories Should We Tell
Example Family Member: Grandpa Slim Allen
Story Ideas: How he lost his front teeth in the Rodeo; The dangers of being a ditch runner; Hardships in the family move from Texas
Family Member:
Family Member:
Family Member:
Family Member:

A Place for Notes, Ideas and Activities

Count Your Blessing on Every Line
I feel blessed because:
I feel blessed because:
I feel blessed because:
I feel blessed because:
I feel blessed because:
I feel blessed because:
I feel blessed because:
I feel blessed because:
I feel blessed because:
I feel blessed because: